D1326933

WWW.SCIENCEOFSTRATEGY.COM

THE SCIENCE OF STRATEGY INSTITUTE

BOOK PROGRAMS
Library Memberships
Book Club Memberships
Books and Audios

ON-LINE TRAINING PROGRAMS
The Warrior Class
The Strategy School

ACADEMY OF STRATEGY
On-line Training
The Academy Library
Personalized Advice on Strategy

INSTITUTE SEMINARS AND TRAINING
A Worldwide Network of Trainers
Internal Corporate Licensing

The Ancient
Bing-fa
Martial Arts Strategy

———————

The Science of
Personal Power

by Sun Tzu &
Gary Gagliardi

Clearbridge Publishing
Science of Strategy Institute

Published by
Clearbridge Publishing, a division of the Science of Strategy Institute

FIRST EDITION, first printing
Copyright 2006 Gary Gagliardi

All rights reserved. No part of this book may be reproduced or transmitted in any part or by any means, electronic or mechanical, including photocopying, recording, or by any information storage and retrieval system, without the written permission of the Publisher, except where permitted by law.

Clearbridge Publishing and the Science of Strategy Institute and their logos are the trademarks of Gary Gagliardi.

Printed in China.
Cover graphic design by Gary Gagliardi
Interior graphic design by Dana and Jeff Wincapaw.
Original Chinese calligraphy by Tsai Yung, Green Dragon Arts, www.greendragonarts.com.

Publisher's Cataloging-in-Publication Data
Sun-tzu, 6th cent. B.C.
       [Sun-tzu ping fa, English]
       The ancient bing-fa: martial arts strategy / Sun Tzu; Gary Gagliardi.
       p. 192 cm. 23
       Includes glossary of key Chinese concepts
       ISBN 1-929194-38-2; IBSN-13 978-1-929194-38-4 (hardcover)
       1. Military art and science - Early works to 1800. 2.Martial arts. 3. Hand-to-hand fighting, Oriental.. I. Gagliardi, Gary 1951— . II. Title.
                           Library of Congress Catalog Card Number: 2006902143

Clearbridge Publishing's books may be purchased for business, for any promotional use, or for special sales. Please contact:

The Science of Strategy Institute
Clearbridge Publishing
PO Box 33772, Seattle, WA 98133
Phone: (206)533-9357 Fax: (206)546-9756
www.scienceofstrategy.com
info@clearbridge.com

Contents

The Ancient *Bing-fa* Martial Arts Strategy

Introduction

Origins of the Martial Arts

Unlike other sports and exercise programs, the martial arts train the whole person—body, spirit, and mind. Down through the millennia, the knowledge on which the martial arts are based—known in China as the *Bing-fa*—was suppressed. Today, most of those who practice martial arts are unfamiliar with these principles except in how they have become embodied in martial arts practice.

The purpose of this book is to explain the secrets of that knowledge. If you practice the martial arts, reading this book will give you a deeper insight into the many aspects of your art. Even if you do not practice the martial arts, learning the concepts on which the martial arts were based will give you powerful intellectual tools for becoming more competitive in your everyday life.

Why the Martial Arts Are Special

All physical training arose originally from military training. The martial arts, however, differ from other sports and exercise programs in three ways:

• Martial arts intentionally train the body, spirit, and mind together as a whole.

• Martial arts use a specific strategy aimed at self-defense and self-development that exploits a loophole in the laws of nature.

• Martial arts cultivate not only physical, mental, and spiritual health but personal virtue.

Like other sports, the martial arts promote physical health by externally training the hands, feet, and eyes. Unlike other sports, the martial arts also emphasize internal training. Internal training brings together the strength of the body (*jing*) with the energy of the spirit (*qi*) and the knowledge of the mind (*shen*). (Note: See the glossary starting on page 184 for the key Chinese concepts.) Other physical training focuses on the body. Martial arts shape the whole person, improving every aspect of your life.

The knowledge of strategy (*bing-fa*) connects your will (*yi shi*) with your breathing (*qi xi*) so that the actions of your body create energy (*qi*) that exerts force—both physical force for fighting and mental force for making better decisions faster.

Martial arts are also different because they are designed for self-defense and self-development. They exploit a loophole in the natural law. Nature says that the strong dominate the weak and the quick beat the slow. The martial arts teach that through the use of knowledge and training, a warrior can transform a stronger, faster opponent into a weaker one. These principles enable you to turn your opponents' strengths into weaknesses and find openings that increase your chances of success in any situation.

This loophole was first discovered and explained 2,500 years ago. Though this work has been kept secret for much of the last two thousand years, it offers history's most valuable insights into the science of personal power. Today, we know this work as Sun Tzu's *The Art of War*. That title—like much of what appears in most English translations of the work—is very misleading. The Chinese title is *Sunzi Bing-fa*, which literally means "Master Sun's Martial Arts."

The Power of *Bing-fa*

The most powerful secrets of *Bing-fa* can be used not only in physical defense, but in advancing your position in all aspects of life. As the intellectual foundation for all martial arts, the *Bing-fa* joins bare-handed forms of fighting (*quan*) with those that use weapons and with those that use the mind alone. As Sun Tzu teaches, a great warrior is not one who wins a hundred battles, but one who finds the way to win without fighting a single battle. Studying the *Bing-fa* teaches the practical magic that is the foundation of martial arts and every other success formula taught today.

Martial arts cultivate virtue. The *Bing-fa* teaches a pragmatic approach to success because it recognizes that direct force and aggression are self-defeating. When you push, others naturally push back. In contrast, we describe the methods of the *Bing-fa* as "winning without conflict," because those methods teach us to avoid meeting force with force. Instead, we look for openings that allow us to use the energy around us.

Basic morality is the foundation of the *Bing-fa* and all martial arts. Some behavior is inherently good while other behavior is inherently bad. Training your body, mind, and spirit is good. Neglecting your body, mind, and spirit is bad. Superiors must love their subordinates like their children. Young people must honor and respect their elders. You must treat others with good faith. You must protect strangers from injustice. You must defend your nation and people and save them from danger.

These moral principles are practical rather than religious. Morality works because it gives you personal power, developing both your inner spirit and strengthening your bonds with others.

Why This Knowledge Was Suppressed

For most of the last two thousand years, access to the ancient *Bing-fa* was severely restricted. Its concepts were originally studied broadly throughout China during the beginning of martial arts practice. However, over the centuries, China's ruling dynasties increasingly decided that its information was too valuable and too dangerous to be left in the hands of the common people. As a philosophy that enables the weak to overcome the strong, this training is always a threat to those in power. As a philosophy that teaches the virtue of innovation and change, the *Bing-fa* encourages both evolution and revolution, which endangers those in power.

In ancient China, there were no printing presses. Most common people didn't know how to read or write. This allowed the nobility to control the distribution of the written forms of the *Bing-fa*. Only the ruling nobility was allowed access to the original text. While its concepts were still passed on in the oral and physical tradition of the martial arts—as they are today—the Chinese emperors themselves took an active role in burying the specifics of this knowledge under layers of safer Asian philosophies, primarily those of Taoism and Zen Buddhism.

Perhaps more importantly, the knowledge of the *Bing-fa* was actively restricted and suppressed. Even today, people from Chinese families tell us that family members warned them that studying the *Bing-fa* was dangerous because the powers that be did not want others to learn its secrets.

Much of this secrecy comes from the lessons of the *Bing-fa* itself. They teach that knowledge and information are the most powerful weapon of all. The *Bing-fa* teaches you how to discover your opponents' secrets and leverage their intentions against them. The *Bing-fa* and the martial arts train the eyes to see what others do not see, using knowledge others do not have.

Given this philosophy, it was only natural that those who mastered *Bing-fa* would want to keep its methods a secret.

The History of Martial Arts Strategy

In China, the martial arts are known today as *Wushu*, but martial arts have gone by many different names in the past. They have been known as *Ji ji* (striking techniques), *Wuyi* (martial arts), *Guoshu* (national technique), and *Gongfu* (practicing techniques), with a host of other names describing specific practices and schools. While names and physical focus of the martial arts have evolved, its underlying philosophy has remained the same. The tradition on which that philosophy is based began over three thousand years ago.

In the eleventh century B.C., King Wen of Zhou wrote the *I Ching*, the root book on Chinese philosophy. This work described *yin* and *yang* as the source of all things in the universe. The work said that the interaction of *gang* (hardness) and *rou* (softness) results in everlasting movement and change. The *I Ching* gave rise to the *ba gua* ("eight ways"). The "before heaven" (*xian tian ba gua*) and "after heaven" (*hou tian ba gua*) diagrams were later used to illustrate the relationships among the key elements in nature. (These diagrams were also used, in a unique form, as the basis for the science of strategy developed later in the *Bing-fa*.) By the eighth century B.C., the first references to the five elements (*wu xing*) of earth, metal, wood, water, and fire appeared.

The first recorded instance of martial arts as a form of personal virtue took place in 659 B.C. Prince Lu captured Lu Na, a local rival. They both dismissed their troops to settle their war by fighting personally, hand to hand (*xiang bo*). They recognized that their supporters should not have to die to settle a disagreement between them. This act elevated the virtue of individual fighting skills but it was not based on an underlying philosophy or strategic viewpoint.

Then in 512 B.C., Sun Wu of Qi (later known as Sun Tzu, that is Master Sun) wrote the *Bing-fa*, history's first scientific description of competitive strategy. If this philosophy hadn't proven so successful, it probably would have been forgotten, but Sun Wu was hired by the kingdom of Wu, a semibarbaric kingdom on the wrong side of the Yangtze River. Wu rose to dominance among the states of pre-empire China. This ended the Autumn and Spring Period of Chinese history and began the Warring States Period (475–221

B.C.). During this era, all the warring states of China were eventually unified.

Master Sun (*Sunzi* in modern Pinyin but *Sun Tzu* traditionally in English) was the first to describe the martial arts primarily as being an intellectual activity depending on character as much as a physical activity. He was the first general to teach that training was what shaped a warrior rather than heritage or pure physical abilities.

Sun Tzu's passion for training infected the king of Wu himself, who became a devotee of sword practice. The king's example spread the popularity of sword training. This led Ma Yuan, a historian of the times, to describe the popularity of sword training as almost a mania, observing in the *Wuyue Chunqiu* (*Annals of the Yue State*) that "A lot of people have been wounded from swords and have scars."

Sun Tzu's view of competitive training led him to recruit and organize the first Chinese citizen army. With it, he conquered most of the Yangtze River valley. He opposed professional, aristocratic forces, many of them hereditary mercenaries. Sun Tzu himself came from a family of landless nobility who specialized in the military arts.

Sun Tzu's success led to the emulation of his methods throughout the states of China, even after his death. The use of citizen armies created wide access to weapons and martial arts training. Professional mercenary families gave rise to history's first professional martial artists. The first such martial artists are introduced in the *Spring and Summer Annals of Wu and Yue* when the old man Yuan Gong met the young swordswoman Yue Nu in battle. These early martial artists eventually became demigods in the Chinese pantheon.

As predicted by Sun Tzu, success in the martial arts also leads to economic success. Around 298 B.C., the historian Zhuang Zi recorded that life in the state of Zhoa had become prosperous because of the practice of martial arts using the sword. King Wen of Zhoa invited more than three thousand sword martial artists to practice against one another in his court. This increased the competition for skilled fighters. Inspired by the Zhoa example, Lord Meng Chang of Qi invited more than sixty thousand martial arts families to stay with him in his fief of Xue in 294 B.C. Hundreds and perhaps thousands were wounded or killed—not in battle, but in simply practicing the quickly evolving art of sword fighting.

Zhuang Zi said that Sun Tzu's theory had been incorporated into the martial arts techniques of both offense and defense and of both armed and unarmed combat. Sun Tzu's ideas were the fundamental principles in the *Book of Sword Fighting* and *Internal Boxing* (*Nei kia Quan*), both published late in the Warring States Period.

Sun Tzu's methods, originally taught in the context of larger wars, were now seen as the key to individual contests. In armed contest, Sun Tzu's lessons on positioning (Chapter Four) are echoed in Zhuang Zi's description of the key methods used.

"The best sword-fighters," he wrote, "pretended to be without preparation as if offering an opening to the enemy. They then gained mastery by striking only after the enemy has struck."

In commenting on bare-handed fighting (*shou bo*), Zhuang Zi echoes Sun Tzu's lessons on momentum (Chapter Five).

"One finds that those who fight with clever techniques initially fight in the ordinary ways," he wrote. "They then change the fighting techniques into tricky methods, even developing them further into ingenious methods."

The fact that Zhuang Zi's descriptions so closely echo Sun Tzu's original formulas for strategy from hundreds of years earlier is unlikely to be a coincidence. We can reasonably deduce that written versions of the *Bing-fa*, or at least parts of it, were known among the educated people of the period. Sun Tzu's descendent, Sun Bing, also popularized the work, and is said to have expanded it from the original thirteen chapters to eighty-two chapters, though unlike the

Bing-fa, surviving parts of Sun Bing's work are less than convincing.

What there is little doubt about is that during this period, knowledge of the *Bing-fa* was widespread. There were even some complaints that the individual fighting of martial arts was interfering with good practice on the battlefield. Strategy became so important in martial arts that Han Fei Zi criticized these new methods as "infringing upon the rules [of war]."

By 221 B.C., the first Qin emperor, Ying Zheng, united the warring kingdoms of China. Changing his name to Qin Shi Huangdi, he also became the first Chinese emperor to attempt to stamp out the widespread development of weapons skills, martial arts, and specifically the knowledge of the *Bing-fa*. Huangdi's burning of books to suppress knowledge is famous, but, according to *The Records of the Historian,* he also collected all the weapons from the citizenry and had them made into bronze bells and twelve giant statues, each weighing two hundred tons. However, all this eventually accomplished was to accelerate the replacement of these weapons with the newer, more modern iron weapons.

After Qin Shi Huangdi, the following Chinese emperors and dynasties alternated between suppressing and promoting the martial arts, but the actual text of the *Bing-fa* was restricted to nobility. The first Han dynasty emperor, Wu, who took control of China in 133 B.C., was a promoter of the martial arts. According to the *Book of the Han Dynasty*, Wu held huge public performances of unarmed combat. Emperor Wu also spread the martial arts to Japan. According to the *Chronicle of Japanese Sports Materials*, the thirty Japanese states that were allied with the Han brought back both sword fighting and bare-handed techniques from China.

In A.D. 82, Ban Gu compiled the *Book of the Han Dynasty*, which categorized books on the art of war into four sections: tactics, features, *yin* and *yang*, and techniques. For the first time, special works on martial arts appeared in the form of thirty-eight treatises on sword-practicing, six on unarmed combat (*shou bo*) and methods for shooting crossbows.

After this period, Taoism became the most popular philosophy in China. In A.D. 126, the disciples of Yu Ji presented a hundred and seventy scrolls on Taoism to Emperor Shun of the Han. While manuscripts of the *Bing-fa* were kept secret, the related ideas of Taoism were promoted to the general public. Taoism became the "official" face of martial arts philosophy—leading directly to today's schools such as the *Ba Gua Zhang* and *Tai Ji Quan*.

Martial arts passed from generation to generation, accumulating more and more traditions. Around A.D. 220, Hua Tu, a famous doctor, popularized a traditional energy-guiding method based on imitating the postures of animals, called *Wu Qin Xi*. The original five animal forms—the tiger, the deer, the bear, the monkey, and the bird—gave birth to *Qigong* (working with energy) and *Xiang Xing Quan* (imitation unarmed combat).

Buddhism became popular in China in 452, when it was embraced by Emperor Wen Cheng of the Northern Wei. From the beginning, the emperor sought to promote Buddhism through a connection to the martial arts. It was recorded by Xu Goa Seng Zhuan that both the emperor and his wife were vegetarians who practiced martial arts in the form of *Wuyi* as a health regime.

This initial connection between Buddhism and the martial arts was further promoted by Emperor Xiao Wen, who built the Shoa Lin temple in the Shong Shan Mountains in 495. According to the *Tai Ping Guang Ji*, the Shoa Lin monks originally practiced martial arts as entertainment. When the famous Zen monk Da Mo (Bodhidharma) came to Shoa Lin, dying there in 528, the temple became the center of both *Chan* (Zen) and *Quan* (unarmed combat).

In 618, Emperor Goa Zu of the Tang Dynasty solicited help from the monks of Sho Lin to fight against the Wang Shichong after they captured the emperor's nephew. Their success led to both financial rewards and further promotion of Buddhism in connection with the martial arts.

As we can see from this gradual transformation, the concepts of the *Bing-fa* were firmly embedded in the origins of the martial arts but gradually covered up. Through their first few hundred years of practice, martial arts embodied the strategy of the *Bing-fa* physically, spiritually, and intellectually. Starting over two thousand years ago, with the first emperor of China, access to the written *Bing-fa* itself was restricted. The pragmatic, revolutionary philosophy taught by the *Bing-fa* was systematically replaced by the less troublesome philosophies of Taoism and Zen Buddhism.

The Rediscovery of the *Bing-Fa*

For thousands of years, until the opening of China to the West, the *Bing-fa* was known only to China's ruling classes. Then a Jesuit missionary, Father Amiot, was given a copy of the text by one of China's princes. In 1782, he published a French translation in Paris. This was the beginning of the general discovery of the *Bing-fa*.

In the past few hundred years, fragmentary versions of the *Bing-fa* have emerged from China. Only in the last few decades have more complete versions been recreated by compiling these different versions and comparing them to recent archeological finds. Not surprisingly, whenever new ancient tombs of Chinese emperors and princes are found, portions of the *Bing-fa* are almost always found buried with them.

Today, the Science of Strategy Institute is at the forefront of uncovering this long-lost knowledge. Our research into the secrets of the *Bing-fa* uncovered its connections with the martial arts. The purpose of this book is to put those who love the martial arts back in touch with the powerful intellectual roots of their training.

The Purpose of This Book

Like all of the works published by the Science of Strategy Institute, the central purpose of this book is to make principles of strategy, as embodied in the ancient *Bing-fa* easy for you to use in your everyday life. However, since we are creating this work specifically for those who practice Asian martial arts, we also seek to put you in touch with the ancient Chinese conceptual framework laid out in the *Bing-fa* that provided the basis for martial arts philosophy.

The Science of Strategy Institute is the world's leading organization in exploring all the uses of the *Bing-fa*. Some of our institute members and our worldwide network trainers both practice and teach the martial arts. Rather than discuss the philosophical differences between the various schools, such as the distinctions made among the three orthodox Chinese schools of unarmed combat, *Xing Yi Quan*, *Tai Ji Quan*, and *Ba Gua Zhang*, we decided that it would be more productive to explain the strategic roots of all Asian martial arts schools. Most of the differences among these schools arose from the later influences of Taoism and Buddhism. It is more productive to discuss the strategic philosophy shared by all martial arts schools rather than the religious differences that divide them.

The design of this book follows that of many of our other works based on Sun Tzu's *The Art of War*. Our English translation of the *Bing-fa*, that is, *The Art of War,* appears on the book's left-hand pages. On the facing right-hand pages, we explain the *Bing-fa*'s ideas in a way that those who practice the martial arts will find most valuable.

Our English translation comes line by line from our award-winning work explaining the original Chinese in *The Art of War Plus the Ancient Chinese Revealed*. Our work in perfecting the translation of the ancient Chinese is internationally recognized. It is so extensive that our books are used today as the basis of translations of Sun Tzu's work into other languages, even Asian languages.

As we explain in our other works, no English translation of the *Bing-fa* can be complete. The original was not written in sentences with one meaning. It is closer in design to mathematical equations that have a variety of uses and applications. Any translation of the original is merely an adaptation of those principles.

While the *Bing-fa* is usually translated in terms of armies at war, that translation is just one adaptation of the original concepts involved. As we show in our glossary, each character in the original is a precise concept, but each concept has a range of meanings and applications, depending on the particular context in which it is used. In creating this special version, we created an English version of the *Bing-fa* that is complete and accurate and replicates how a martial artist of the Warring States Period would have understood the book's lessons in strategy. This understanding is the conceptual basis for all martial arts.

On the facing right-hand pages, we explain each stanza of the original text in the specific context of mastering martial arts strategy. Sun Tzu did not write his lessons for the uninitiated, but for a person who had learned the underlying principles from a living master and cultural traditions. In our explanation, we simply discuss what a warrior of the period would have known that you cannot know. In certain cases, this means we explain certain Chinese concepts in more detail. In other cases, we illustrate the concepts involved with examples of how they are used in modern martial arts.

We think that after reading this work, you will agree that no education in the martial arts is truly complete without an understanding of its philosophical foundations.

The *Ba Gua*

Chapter 1

Analysis: Know the Key Factors

This chapter focuses on strategic analysis or, more precisely, the analysis of strategic positions. In studying martial arts, most students learn to see different aspects of the art as the halves of a larger whole. This division is discussed in terms of *yin* and *yang*, defense and attack, inhale and exhale, close and open, soft and hard, and so on. In the *Bing-fa* these "complementary opposites" are only part of a larger picture. Strategic analysis requires understanding the relationships among different groups of complementary opposites.

The first and most important group are five key factors defining a strategic position. These five factors are philosophy, climate, ground, methods, and the leader. Climate and ground (heaven and earth) are complementary opposites, as are the leader and methods (decisions and actions). These two sets of balancing opposites are grouped around the central core of philosophy.

These five factors are the original pattern of five used throughout the martial arts. There are five types of weapons (airborne, long, short, soft, and double), five original animal forms (tiger, deer, bear, monkey, and bird), and five types of punches (*pi, beng, zuan, pao,* and *heng*). All are related to the five physical elements (*wu xing*) of earth, metal, wood, water, and fire.

As you will see, these patterns of five in the *Bing-fa* are all connected to each other and to the larger pattern of nine that comes out of the *ba gua* (its eight sides and center).

Analysis

SUN TZU SAID:

This is war. 1
It is the most important skill in the nation.
It is the basis of life and death.
It is the philosophy of survival or destruction.
You must know it well.

6Your skill comes from five factors.
Study these factors when you plan war.
You must insist on knowing your situation.
1.	Discuss philosophy.
2.	Discuss the climate.
3.	Discuss the ground.
4.	Discuss leadership.
5.	Discuss martial methods.

14It starts with your martial philosophy.
Command your people in a way that gives them a higher
shared purpose.
You can lead them to death.
You can lead them to life.
They must never fear danger or dishonesty.

Know the Key Factors

THE MARTIAL ARTIST HEARS:

1 The term translated as "war" is *bing*, which is better understood as "martial strategy." The foundation of martial arts was military training for defense of the nation. Today, of course, we think more about personal defense, but the mastery of these skills is still a matter of life or death, and success or failure.

Sun Tzu teaches that success in using strategy depends on your unique strategic position. He defines that position using five concepts. The Chinese terms for these are:

1. *Tao*: literally "way," meaning underlying motivation or direction
2. *Tian*: literally "heaven," meaning the trends in time
3. *Di*: the "ground" on which you compete
4. *Jiang*: the "general," but meaning the leader or decision-maker
5. *Fa*: your "methods," which include your procedures and systems

The central component of your position is the concept of *tao*, which means "way" or "philosophy." You can win respect from others only on the basis of sharing their goals and ideals.

Some values are worth dying for. Some values make life worth living. If others have nothing to fear from you and trust you, your position creates supporters instead of opponents.

[19]Next, you have the climate.
It can be sunny or overcast.
It can be hot or cold.
It includes the timing of the seasons.

[23]Next is the terrain.
It can be distant or near.
It can be difficult or easy.
It can be open or narrow.
It also determines your life or death.

[28]Next is the commander.
He must be smart, trustworthy, caring, brave, and strict.

[30]Finally, you have your martial methods.
They shape your organization.
They come from your controlling philosophy.
You must master their use.

[34]All five of these factors are critical.
As a commander, you must pay attention to them.
Understanding them brings victory.
Ignoring them means defeat.

The climate is *tian*, which means "sky" or "heaven." The climate embodies changes that you cannot control and that shift between extremes. The future looks bright or dismal. Your luck runs hot or cold. You find patterns or trends in these changes that you can use.

The terrain or ground, *di* in Chinese, is both where you fight and what you fight to win. However, *di* also means condition and situation—that is, how you are placed or situated, for example, your standing in a school or society. *Di* also has an economic component. The ground is the source of your financial resources.

A leader's character connects the five factors: smart–ground, trust–leadership, caring–philosophy, brave–climate, and strict–methods.

There are dozens of schools of martial arts, each teaching different types of methods. Each school is formed by its methods. A school only survives if it is true to its philosophy. Notice that mastering these skills is only one part of your strategic position.

These five key elements are extensively defined in the course of this work. Each chapter focuses on one or more of these elements. Martial arts strategy is the intellectual component of martial arts training. Technical skill is wasted without this strategic skill.

You must learn through planning. 2
You must question the situation.

³You must ask:
Which government has the right philosophy?
Which commander has the skill?
Which season and place has the advantage?
Which method of command works?
Which group of forces has the strength?
Which officers and men have the training?
Which rewards and punishments make sense?
This tells when you will win and when you will lose.
Some commanders perform this analysis.
If you use these commanders, you will win.
Keep them.
Some commanders ignore this analysis.
If you use these commanders, you will lose.
Get rid of them.

Plan an advantage by listening. 3
Adjust to the situation.
Get assistance from the outside.
Influence events.
Then planning can find opportunities and give you control.

2 The concept is *xiao*, which is translated as "learn," but it also means "compare" and "double-check."

Martial arts strategy requires you to compare your position with that of others. This develops a realistic perspective. You can never say how "good" anything is without comparing it to an existing example—for example, other martial artists. You must constantly compare your philosophy, how you are changing, your situation, your character, and your technical abilities with those of others. This comparative analysis allows you to match your strengths against an opponent's weaknesses. This alone lets you choose among a number of possible actions.

The best martial arts teachers are constantly comparing the skills of their students in each of these areas. These are the people with whom you want to train.

Some martial arts trainers fail to judge their students' skills objectively. These teachers are not going to do you any good. You must move on to a better teacher.

3 The foundation of strategy is knowledge (*zhi*), but the base of knowledge is listening to others, especially those with outside viewpoints. You must continually open yourself to new ideas that come in from outside your normal channels of information. This new information is the source of opportunity (*li*).

Warfare is one thing. 4
It is a philosophy of deception.

3When you are ready, you try to appear incapacitated.
When active, you pretend inactivity.
When you are close to the enemy, you appear distant.
When far away, you pretend you are near.

7You can have an advantage and still entice an opponent.
You can be disorganized and still be decisive.
You can be ready and still be preparing.
You can be strong and still avoid battle.
You can be angry and still stop yourself.
You can humble yourself and still be confident.
You can be relaxed and still be working.
You can be close to an ally and still part ways.
You can attack a place without planning to do so.
You can leave a place without giving away your plan.

17You will find a place where you can win.
You cannot first signal your intentions.

4 The Chinese term *gui* is translated as "deception," but it means using misleading actions, feinting, and bluffing.

In martial arts competition, ignorance is safer than the illusion of knowledge. Over two thousand years ago, the Chinese historian Zhuang Zi observed that what made the skilled martial artist different from other fighters was his focus on misleading opponents.

Deception (*gui*) controls perceptions. Deception or illusion is an attack on vision, creating a false opportunity or a false threat. Even though you know your own condition, your opponents do not. They only know what you do. The martial arts are like poker. Opponents don't know what your cards are. They only know how you act. You act as if you are going to do one thing so that you can do another. To bluff successfully you cannot always be predictable. To mislead others you do things that you don't need to do. You must keep your opponents guessing about your real strengths, weaknesses, and intentions.

Success depends on establishing a position that others cannot attack. People will block you if they know where you are moving.

Manage to avoid battle until your side can count on 5
certain victory.
You must calculate many advantages.
Before you go to battle, your organization's analysis can indi-
cate that you may not win.
You can count few advantages.
Many advantages add up to victory.
Few advantages add up to defeat.
How can you know your advantages without analyzing them?
We can see where we are by means of our observations.
We can foresee our victory or defeat by planning.

5 You must be patient enough to wait until the odds are all in your favor. You must choose paths that offer many opportunities. This is why you constantly analyze your position. You have to recognize when an objective analysis indicates that you may lose. If your success is uncertain, prior analysis will foresee the problem. You must avoid situations that offer fewer certain opportunities.

Choices that open up more opportunities lead to success.

Choices that eliminate opportunities lead to failure.

How can you see your opportunities without analysis? Martial artists train themselves to see their situation as it truly is. This is how you create success and prevent failure.

Chapter 2

Going to War: Conserve Your Resources

In his second chapter, Sun Tzu discusses the cost of competition and the price of failure. When you meet another in battle, your actions cost time and energy. Your internal resources are limited. The magic of *Bing-fa* is that martial force enables you to avoid wasting your time and energy by making the right choices.

This chapter begins by discussing the price of failure. The path of the martial artist is not painless. Martial artists realize that every action they take has a cost attached to it. Regular people are blissfully unaware of the costs of their decisions. As a martial artist, you must learn to appreciate the harsh reality of unavoidable costs in the face of limited resources.

Sun Tzu's *Bing-fa* balances costs with potential rewards. Sun Tzu teaches the economics of conservation. A martial artist learns to evaluate every potential move based on its investment in effort, time, and space. The bigger, more time-consuming, and more distant a strike is, the most costly and risky it is. For this reason, Sun Tzu teaches you to attack forward in small, quick, close moves. Small movements are more powerful because they are less risky.

The second part of choosing the right path is identifying openings that give you more in advantages than they consume in effort. Some paths can save you effort, time, and space. You can identify and put your efforts into openings that increase your leverage and strength over time. Martial artists identify and invest in efforts that give them more resources relative to their opponents.

Going to War

SUN TZU SAID:

Everything depends on your use of martial philosophy. 1
Moving the army requires thousands of vehicles.
These vehicles must be loaded thousands of times.
The army must carry a huge supply of arms.
You need ten thousand acres of grain.
This results in internal and external shortages.
Any army consumes resources like an invader.
It uses up glue and paint for wood.
It requires armor for its vehicles.
People complain about the waste of a vast amount of metal.
It will set you back when you attempt to raise tens of thousands of troops.

[12]Using a huge force makes war very expensive to win.
Long delays create a dull army and sharp defeats.
Attacking enemy cities drains your forces.
Long violent campaigns that exhaust the nation's resources
are wrong.

Conserve Your Resources

THE MARTIAL ARTIST HEARS:

1 This chapter discusses your goals in the context of the costs involved. Though Sun Tzu phrases these ideas in terms of marshalling a military force, as a martial artist you must see these in terms of the personal costs of making decisions. Every decision you make has costs associated with it. Your choices commit your time and effort in a specific direction. You need enough resources to satisfy your needs. Your mental and physical assets are limited. Any endeavor can demand more resources than it is worth. Your existing position requires protection as you move forward. You have to worry about what every effort will cost you. Focusing your energy in unnecessary directions consumes more resources than these efforts can return.

The *Bing-fa* teaches you to think mathematically about the cost of your efforts. The cost of making a commitment is determined by the size of that effort multiplied by its duration. Committing to long-term projects requires planning that can stifle your progress. Setting oversized goals that are beyond your ability leads to failure.

¹⁶Manage a dull army.
You will suffer sharp defeats.
You will drain your forces.
Your money will be used up.
Your rivals will multiply as your army collapses and they will
begin against you.
It doesn't matter how smart you are.
You cannot get ahead by taking losses!

²³You hear of people going to battle too quickly.
Still, you won't see a skilled battle that lasts a long time.

²⁵You can fight a war for a long time or you can make your
nation strong.
You can't do both.

Make no assumptions about all the dangers in using 2
martial force.
Then you won't make assumptions about the benefits of
using arms either.

³You want to make good use of war.
Do not raise troops repeatedly.
Do not carry too many supplies.
Choose to be useful to your nation.
Feed off the enemy.
Make your army carry only the provisions it needs.

For a true martial artist who makes life-and-death decisions, the problem isn't simply taking risks and failing. You can't afford to make costly mistakes from which you cannot recover. Even when the competition is just economic, you survive only as long as you have money to continue. When you have resources, you have allies. When you lack resources, the world turns its back on you. Our first priority in competitive action is to preserve our financial strength. We can never afford to spend our way to success.

A true martial artist never jumps into a situation without considering its costs. Any well-fought match is over quickly.

You can plan long, drawn-out, costly matches or you can develop moves that decide matches quickly. The first frame of mind prohibits the latter.

2 A true martial artist never pretends that he or she knows all the risks in choosing a course of action. Competition is the realm of chaos. Competition will bring you both more or less success than you expect. Wisdom comes only from trying.

In a match, you choose your actions carefully. You do not have an infinite amount of energy. You cannot afford to correct your mistakes. You cannot afford a lot of excess baggage. Choose what is good for your body. Accept the openings and energy that your opponents give you. The less you expend in effort, the more quickly your efforts can become successful.

The nation impoverishes itself shipping to troops that 3
are far away.
Distant transportation is costly for hundreds of families.
Buying goods with the army nearby is also expensive.
High prices also exhaust wealth.
If you exhaust your wealth, you then quickly hollow out your
military.
Martial forces consume a nation's wealth entirely.
War leaves households in the former heart of the nation
with nothing.

[8]War destroys hundreds of families.
Out of every ten families, war leaves only seven.
War empties the government's storehouses.
Broken armies will get rid of their horses.
They will throw down their armor, helmets, and arrows.
They will lose their swords and shields.
They will leave their wagons without oxen.
War will consume 60 percent of everything you have.

Because of this, it is the intelligent commander's duty to 4
feed off the enemy.

[2]Use a cup of the enemy's food.
It is worth twenty of your own.
Win a bushel of the enemy's feed.
It is worth twenty of your own.

3 Here the *Bing-fa* adds a third dimension of cost to size and time, the dimension of distance. Though Sun Tzu discusses the problem of the cost of distance in terms of transporting an army, the first martial artists read it differently. In combat, the more physical distance a move requires, the more energy it takes and the more time it takes. Both increase the danger of making such a move. Big moves are impressive for show, but they are also expensive in combat. In terms of knowledge, this rule means specialization. Martial artists who move too far from the forms they know find that they are poorer for it.

The life of the warrior is inherently dangerous. Competition is dangerous and painful. Most competitors are unsuccessful most of the time. Many of your attempts at improving your position are doomed to failure. Don't risk your future mobility on the possibility of failure. You must maintain the ability to defend your position. Successful fighters always know how to husband their resources. They always protect their ability to move. They keep movements small, quick, and close to minimize costs.

4 The challenge of husbanding your resources means you must use your opponents' resources against them.

Martial artists feed off their enemy's strength. Energy and momentum that you win from your opponents are worth twenty times more than resources that you bring to a contest. Martial arts focus on leveraging an opponent's moves against him or her.

⁶You can kill the enemy and frustrate him as well.
Take the enemy's strength from him by stealing away his
money.

⁸Fight for the enemy's supply wagons.
Capture his supplies by using overwhelming force.
Reward the first who capture them.
Then change their banners and flags.
Mix them in with your own wagons to increase your supply
line.
Keep your forces strong by providing for them.
This is what it means to beat the enemy while you grow
more powerful.

Make victory in war pay for itself. 5
Avoid expensive, long campaigns.
The martial commander's knowledge is the key.
It determines whether the civilian officials can govern.
It determines whether the nation's households are peaceful
or a danger to the state.

✦ ✦ ✦

In a match, frustrating your opponent is as important as beating him or her. When you steal away your opponent's strength, you deplete his or her emotional resources.

Fight to deplete the internal resources your opponents need to continue. For example, you can make it difficult for opponents to get their breath. You are quickly rewarded when you deprive your opponents of the resources they require. As they are weakened, you automatically increase the relative supply of your own internal resources and the stamina you need to keep going.

Your physical strength will increase as your confidence of eventual success increases. The best martial artists advance their positions in ways that give them more resources to draw upon.

5 In the practice of martial arts, your work must increase your resources. Make the least costly choices as you move toward your goals. The key to controlling costs is your knowledge. The more knowledge of cost control you exhibit, the easier it is to win decisions from the judges. Knowledge allows you to reap the rewards of training and avoid the costs of competition.

Chapter 3

Planning an Attack: Unite for Focus and Speed

The philosophy of martial arts views the human body as a smaller universe within the larger universe of nature. The same laws govern both. The laws of strategy in the *Bing-fa* are scalable, which means they work at any level of organization, from a single person to a large organization.

From the time of the *Bing-fa*, the goal of martial arts is to put the body in tune with this natural law. Martial arts are a form of holistic health. They seek to bridge the division between the internal and the external world. The study of the lessons of *Bing-fa* does for your mind what the physical training of martial arts does for your body. As you grow in understanding of how your mind and body work, you also grow in understanding of how the world works.

The topic of this chapter is unity and focus. The goal of unity and focus is not to win confrontations but to develop positions that others cannot attack. Most of this chapter deals with facing groups of opponents. The worst way to deal with rivals is to attack them when they are concentrated in a large group.

In the face of opposition, you use small, focused actions in which you or your group has a clear advantage. The relative size of competing groups determines the type of action you choose. Political divisions undermine the strength of a group. A divided group loses its focus. Groups need leaders. Leaders need certain types of knowledge and skill to make good decisions. You must join groups with good leadership. Leaders are judged by their knowledge.

Planning an Attack

SUN TZU SAID:

Everyone relies on the arts of war. 1
A united nation is strong.
A divided nation is weak.
A united army is strong.
A divided army is weak.
A united force is strong.
A divided force is weak.
United men are strong.
Divided men are weak.
A united unit is strong.
A divided unit is weak.

[12]Unity works because it enables you to win every battle you
fight.
Still, this is the foolish goal of a weak leader.
Avoid battle and make the enemy's men surrender.
This is the right goal for a superior leader.

The best way to make war is to ruin the enemy's plans. 2
The next best is to disrupt alliances.
The next best is to attack the opposing army.
The worst is to attack the enemy's cities.

Unite for Focus and Speed

1 There has always been a tension within martial arts between the individual and the larger group. As early as the third century A.D., writers complained about how individual goals interfered with good teamwork. The *Bing-fa* addresses this issue. The Chinese term *muo* is translated as "united," but its meaning is closer to "complete" or "whole." Its complementary opposite is *po*, which is translated as "divided" but means literally "broken" or "worn out." Cohesion within a group is the source of strength. A group is strong only when it has a core of strongly shared values, or *tao*. However, the unity of any large group is only as good as the unity of its various parts, down to the unity of the individual in mind and body.

Regular people join larger groups because they feel weak and they are concerned about succeeding in conflict with others. The *Bing-fa* teaches a deeper lesson. Being part of a group is a way of avoiding conflict, a way of not only getting others to surrender but to join you. Groups bring together knowledge into schools.

2 Martial artists first use *gui*, that is, misdirection, to make it difficult for opponents to act. They then focus on dividing the groups allied against them. Only then do they meet others in battle. Martial artists avoid attacking solid, fortified positions directly.

⁵This is what happens when you attack a city.

You can attempt it, but you can't finish it.

First you must make siege engines.

You need the right equipment and machinery.

It takes three months and still you cannot win.

Then you try to encircle the area.

You use three more months without making progress.

Your command still doesn't succeed and this angers you.

You then try to swarm the city.

This kills a third of your officers and men.

You are still unable to draw the enemy out of the city.

This attack is a disaster.

Make good use of war. 3

Make the enemy's troops surrender.

You can do this fighting only minor battles.

You can draw their men out of their cities.

You can do it with small attacks.

You can destroy the men of a nation.

You must keep your campaign short.

⁸You must use total war, fighting with everything you have.

Never stop fighting when at war.

You can gain complete advantage.

To do this, you must plan your strategy of attack.

Though the *Bing-fa* discusses attacking strong positions in terms of attacking cities, the psychological lessons apply to any scale of conflict. People want what others have. Fighters attempt to prove their superiority by attacking the strengths of opponents rather than their weaknesses. Human ego passes through a predictable cycle of thoughts and emotions in these attacks. It starts with thinking that you can win by planning. When this doesn't work, you hope to find an opening through patience. In the end, however, both planning and patience are exhausted. At this point, emotion takes over. At this point, you react instinctively, trying to overpower opponents by using force. The whole point of learning strategy is to avoid this destructive and pointless exercise.

3 When you are planning a competitive strategy, you look for openings where opponents cannot resist you. You use your position to destroy your opponents' will to fight. You do this one small step at a time. You can lure opponents to move away from their strengths with small intrusions into their unprotected space. This approach eventually undermines the strongest opponents. Acting quickly keeps them off balance.

You always focus all your energies on using every opening. You constantly work your opponents, trying to take them out of position. They eventually make a mistake that gives you a decisive advantage. You look for openings focusing on their weaknesses.

¹²The rules for making war are:
If you outnumber enemy forces ten to one, surround them.
If you outnumber them five to one, attack them.
If you outnumber them two to one, divide them.
If you are equal, then find an advantageous battle.
If you are fewer, defend against them.
If you are much weaker, evade them.

¹⁹Small forces are not powerful.
However, large forces cannot catch them.

You must master command. 4
The nation must support you.

³Supporting the military makes the nation powerful.
Not supporting the military makes the nation weak.

⁵The army's position is made more difficult by politicians in
three different ways.
Ignorant of the whole army's inability to advance, they order
an advance.
Ignorant of the whole army's inability to withdraw, they
order a withdrawal.
We call this tying up the army.
Politicians don't understand the army's business.
Still, they think they can run an army.
This confuses the army's officers.

The *Bing-fa* teaches that size is not the source of strength. Force (*shi*) comes from your ability to concentrate your efforts at the right point at the right moment. Your tactics during a contest depend entirely upon the immediate balance of force. Ideally, you can completely dominate your opponent. When this is not possible, you act according to your relative strength: you divide their efforts, pick your places, defend your strong points, or avoid contact accordingly.

Size is both an advantage and a disadvantage. Large can overpower small, but small can move more quickly than large.

4 As a martial artist, know how to lead others. You must know how to win the support of your companions.

Having the support of others makes you powerful.
Not having the support of others makes you weak.

The martial force of a group is undermined by group members who want to play on the divisions within the group. Divided groups can act to hurt the whole group for the benefit of one part of the group. Divided groups also act to protect some members to the detriment of the group as a whole. Internal politics divide many groups, both those of your supporters and your opponents. People within divided groups are always hamstrung. Those who work to improve their position within a group by dividing it fail to understand the goals of teamwork. These politicians destroy the group's focus on its mission. They make decision-making difficult.

[12]Politicians don't know the army's chain of command.
They give the army too much freedom.
This will create distrust among the army's officers.

[15]The entire army becomes confused and distrusting.
This invites invasion by many different rivals.
We say correctly that disorder in an army kills victory.

You must know five things to win: 5
Victory comes from knowing when to attack and when to avoid battle.
Victory comes from correctly using both large and small forces.
Victory comes from everyone sharing the same goals.
Victory comes from finding opportunities in problems.
Victory comes from having a capable commander and the government leaving him alone.
You must know these five things.
You then know the theory of victory.

We say: 6
"Know yourself and know your enemy.
You will be safe in every battle.
You may know yourself but not know the enemy.
You will then lose one battle for every one you win.
You may not know yourself or the enemy.
You will then lose every battle."

♦ ♦ ♦

Internal politics confuse any group's priorities. Without shared priorities, everyone seeks to satisfy his or her own individual goals. Everyone loses confidence that the others will support him or her.

A breakdown in a group's unity and focus creates weakness. Weakness in any organization invites competition from other groups. Without unity and focus, no group can be successful.

5 The five key types of knowledge map into the five key elements introduced in the first chapter. Knowing when to meet opponents and, just as importantly, when not to meet them, is based on *tian*, the current trends. Knowing how to use different sized forces is a matter of *fa*, understanding methods. Sharing the same goals requires *tao*, an underlying, uniting mission. Discovering opportunities demands knowledge of *di*, the competitive ground. Finally, the group needs to know who to turn to for the final decision. This is the *jiang*, the general and leader. Strategy pits these five forms of knowledge against the brute force of opponents. Success comes from pitting knowledge of the situation against simple force.

6 Progress starts with listening. You cannot know yourself and how you compare to potential opponents except by getting feedback from others. If you know your relative strength, you can always defend yourself. If you only focus on what you can do, you will lose half your contests. If you are constantly losing, it is because you are deluded about your own abilities and not seeing the abilities of others.

Chapter 4

Positioning: Use Your Form

The Chinese term *xing* translates as "position" or "form." It means
the formation or concentration of efforts around a specific position. According to the science of *Bing-fa*, an offensive move to a new
position should only be made when a clear, certain-to-be-successful
opportunity presents itself.

In the martial arts, this concept of form was organized around
styles emulating animal forms starting in the third century A.D.
The original five animal forms—the tiger, the deer, the bear, the
monkey, and the bird—were expanded into twelve forms with the
advent of *Xing-yi Quan* (form-mind or body-mind boxing). *Xing-yi
Quan* is perhaps the oldest martial arts style still practiced today.
Standard *Xing-yi Quan* consists of the dragon, tiger, horse, monkey,
chicken, harrier, Chinese ostrich, swallow, eagle, bear, water lizard,
and snake. Each form must be understood in terms of its shape
and its purpose. Shape is an aspect of your ground or situation (*di*).
Purpose is an aspect of your philosophy and goals (*tao*).

You make success easy by using your existing position or form
as your springboard to future positions. Regular people tend to
think negatively about their current situation. This negativity
results in a sense of inadequacy and inferiority. Successful fighters
see the unique value in their special position. Warriors are keenly
aware of their own assets. Without a proper appreciation of your
current position and form, you cannot advance that position, move
forward, and master new forms.

Positioning

SUN TZU SAID:

Learn from the history of successful battles. 1
First, you should control the situation, not try to win.
If you adjust to the enemy, you will find a way to win.
The opportunity to win does not come from yourself.
The opportunity to win comes from your enemy.

6You must pick good battles.
You can control them until you can win.
You cannot win them until the enemy enables your victory.

9We say:
You see the opportunity for victory; you don't create it.

Use Your Form

THE MARTIAL ARTIST HEARS:

1 The martial arts all teach that competitive contests are always won because one competitor leaves an opening for the other. Because of this, your first responsibility should be to control your position. You can then adjust to your opponents' positions to utilize openings that they leave. This creates the opportunity to strike successfully.

The Chinese concept *zhan* is translated as "battle." However, it doesn't mean conflict. It means meeting opponents or challenges. You choose a form that holds them until they leave an opening.

A skilled martial artist looks for openings that arise from the dynamics of movement. You don't create your opportunities.

You are sometimes unable to win. 2
You must then defend.
You will eventually be able to win.
You must then attack.
Defend when you have insufficient strength.
Attack when you have a surplus of strength.

7You must defend yourself well.
Save your forces and dig in.
You must attack well.
Move your forces when you have a clear advantage.

11You must always protect yourself until you can completely
triumph.

Some may see how to win. 3
However, they cannot position their forces where they must.
This demonstrates limited ability.

4Some can struggle to a victory and the whole world may
praise their winning.
This also demonstrates a limited ability.

6Win as easily as picking up a fallen hair.
Don't use all of your forces.
See the time to move.
Don't try to find something clever.
Hear the clap of thunder.
Don't try to hear something subtle.

2 Following the *Bing-fa*, decisions about attacking and defending are automatic. You initially use your position and form to defend yourself. You never attack unless you have both an opening and the ability to take advantage of that opening. When your ability is limited, you defend. If you see a clear opportunity, you must attack. Attacking implies moving forward into an opponent's space.

Defense is associated with staying in your position, conserving your energy, and keeping a low profile.

Attack, in contrast, implies movement or action while using an opportunity from a position of strength.

Your success depends upon your ability to protect yourself and survive long enough for an opening to present itself.

3 When an opportunity does present itself, you must recognize it and know how to move to take advantage of the opening. Vision without the ability to act gets you nowhere.

However, finding an opening is critical in martial arts. Some think that the more difficult the struggle the more glorious the success, but, in the martial arts, action without judgment is dangerous.

Sun Tzu teaches that every situation is full of opportunities. You must choose the path of least resistance rather than the path of maximum effort. The "time to move" is when the motion is in your favor. The "clap of thunder" means true openings are clear to the trained fighter. Until you are trained, you must be careful not to imagine opportunities where they do not exist.

¹²Learn from the history of successful battles.
Victory goes to those who make winning easy.
A good battle is one that you will obviously win.
It doesn't take intelligence to win a reputation.
It doesn't take courage to achieve success.

¹⁷You must win your battles without effort.
Avoid difficult struggles.
Fight when your position must win.
You always win by preventing your defeat.

²¹You must engage only in winning battles.
Position yourself where you cannot lose.
Never waste an opportunity to defeat your enemy.

²⁴You win a war by first assuring yourself of victory.
Only afterward do you look for a fight.
Outmaneuver the enemy before the first battle and then
fight to win.

When the *Bing-fa* refers to "history," it looks at what happens over time to lead to eventual success. Easy progress requires picking the right opportunities. An opening is worth exploiting if it gives you an easy victory. People who fight difficult battles to build a reputation are foolish. Only fools look for glory at the expense of success.

The *Bing-fa* doesn't force success. You always win by preventing your defeat. Good defense is the prerequisite for success. It not only allows you to be selective about picking your openings, but it forces opponents to make riskier moves that create openings.

When an opponent eventually leaves you an opening, you must act but your form must not endanger you. When you can attack safely, you can use every opportunity that presents itself.

Strategy focuses on winning over the long term. You look for positions that force opponents to expose their weaknesses. You avoid confrontation until you discover these winning positions. Once you commit yourself to action, you make sure the action is successful.

You must make good use of war. 4
Study martial philosophy and the art of defense.
You can control your victory or defeat.

⁴This is the art of war:
1.　　　　Discuss the distances.
2.　　　　Discuss your numbers.
3.　　　　Discuss your calculations.
4.　　　　Discuss your decisions.
5.　　　　Discuss victory.

¹⁰The ground determines the distance.
The distance determines your numbers.
Your numbers determine your calculations.
Your calculations determine your decisions.
Your decisions determine your victory."

¹⁵Creating a winning war is like balancing a coin of gold
against a coin of silver.
Creating a losing war is like balancing a coin of silver
against a coin of gold.

Winning a battle is always a matter of people. 5
You pour them into battle like a flood of water pouring into
a deep gorge.
This is a matter of positioning.

♦ ♦ ♦

4 Martial artists are trained not to waste their efforts. You must understand the goals of martial arts and focus first on self-defense. Your choices determine what happens to you.

The science of strategy clearly defines an opening or opportunity.
1. Openings are close rather than far.
2. Openings allow you to exert leverage.
3. Openings put opponents at a disadvantage.
4. Openings offer a minimum of risks.
5. Openings give you success.

The distance comes from your current position relative to where the opening is. The greater the distance from you, the less leverage your position gives you. You calculate your opponent's leverage at the opening compared with your own. If you don't see a clear advantage in moving into the opening, you don't move into it.

A competitive contest is dynamic. You can't do everything so you must choose the best openings over those that are good but not great. Over the long term, trying to take advantage of second-rate opportunities adds up to failure.

5 You choose the best positions and the best openings to create momentum, the topic of the next chapter. Putting yourself in the right place at the right time with the right resources is the start of momentum. Without good form, you cannot create momentum.

✦ ✦ ✦

Chapter 5

Momentum: Build the Pressure

Certainly all martial arts study the physical force of momentum. The Japanese forms of the martial arts, in particular *judo*, *ju-jitsu* (*ju* means "gentle"), and *aikido* ("the way of the harmonious spirit") specifically teach the idea of giving way and using the opponent's momentum against him or her. Through movement, the physical momentum of attack is redirected and neutralized.

However, the *Bing-fa* teaches a more sophisticated, psychological concept of momentum. In Chinese, the term is *shi* (force), but it is not just physical force. It means putting people and events into motion in such a way that they become unstoppable. This is the way we use the term "momentum" in a football game or a political contest, where the feeling is that one side is clearly winning.

Sun Tzu teaches that there is a process by which psychological momentum is created. Momentum doesn't come just from winning consistently. Psychological momentum comes from a surprising win. Creating momentum requires starting with a standard, expected move to set up a surprising, unexpected move. Used during the chaos of battle, the prepared surprise increases the sense of chaos for your opponent while increasing your sense of control.

Every contest takes unexpected turns. The key is to prepare your surprises in advance. A martial artist learns how to prepare for changes in direction and to harness them to create momentum. If you are prepared for the unexpected and your opponents are not, you can take control of any situation.

Momentum

SUN TZU SAID:

You control a large group the same as you control a few. 1
You just divide their ranks correctly.
You fight a large army the same as you fight a small one.
You only need the right position and communication.
You may meet a large enemy army.
You must be able to sustain an enemy attack without being
defeated.
You must correctly use both surprise and direct action.
Your army's position must increase your strength.
Troops flanking an enemy can smash them like eggs.
You must correctly use both strength and weakness.

It is the same in all battles. 2
You use a direct approach to engage the enemy.
You use surprise to win.

[4]You must use surprise for a successful invasion.
Surprise is as infinite as the weather and land.
Surprise is as inexhaustible as the flow of a river.

Build the Pressure

1 The *Bing-fa* explains martial arts strategy in terms of armies, but they are the same for a single fighter. You simply have to understand Sun Tzu's points correctly. You defeat larger foes in the same way you defeat smaller ones. You need to use the strength of your position and send the right messages. You will certainly meet larger and stronger opponents. If you understand the rules of momentum, you can survive the opponent's attack long enough to find an opening. You create the winning force, called *shi,* by combining what is expected (*jang*) with what is unexpected (*qi*). Your *xing*—current position—is the source of your unique strengths (*sat*). You leverage that strength or fullness against the opponent's weaknesses (*xu*).

2 Two complementary opposites create *shi*. You cannot win with expected, standard methods, known as *jang,* because opponents prepare for them. You win using the unexpected, called *qi*.

As an attack on expectations, the surprise of *qi* is required to get past an opponent's guard. The unlimited potential of *qi* arises from the infinite variety of ground and constantly changing climate.

7You can be stopped and yet recover the initiative.
You must use your days and months correctly.

9If you are defeated, you can recover.
You must use the four seasons correctly.

11There are only a few notes in the scale.
Yet you can always rearrange them.
You can never hear every song of victory.

14There are only a few basic colors.
Yet you can always mix them.
You can never see all the shades of victory.

17There are only a few flavors.
Yet you can always blend them.
You can never taste all the flavors of victory.

20You fight with momentum.
There are only a few types of surprises and direct actions.
Yet you can always vary the ones you use.
There is no limit to the ways you can win.

24Surprise and direct action give birth to each other.
They are like a circle without end.
You cannot exhaust all their possible combinations!

Surging water flows together rapidly. 3
Its pressure washes away boulders.
This is momentum.

The secret to regaining lost momentum (*shi*) is switching back and forth between the standards of *jang* and the surprise of *qi* over time.

The innovative power of "standard surprises," *jang-qi*, allows you to recover from failure through continuous improvement over time.

Though Sun Tzu's description of rearranging elements to make *jang-qi* innovation is poetic, it represents three steps in a process. The first step is *zhi*, knowledge, symbolized in the *Bing-fa* by listening.

The next step in the creative process is *jian*, that is, vision, which means foresight, inspiration, or taking aim at an opening, which is symbolized by sight.

The final step evaluates the position and action when you act on your vision. This is the idea of testing, tasting, and judging, which is symbolized by flavor or smell.

Success comes from developing *shi*, momentum. *Shi*, in turn, comes from *jang-qi*, combining proven moves in novel ways. You cannot let yourself get caught in the rut of using the same techniques. A few basic moves can be combined in an infinite variety of different ways.

Sun Tzu teaches that innovative moves only arise from well-honed practice and that new standards result only from trials of new moves. Together, they create the infinite variety of innovation.

3 Water is the *Bing-fa*'s metaphor for change. *Shi* (momentum) arising from *jang-qi* ("standard surprise") is a force for eliminating the obstacles that hamper your progress.

4A hawk suddenly strikes a bird.
Its contact alone kills the prey.
This is timing.

7You must fight only winning battles.
Your momentum must be overwhelming.
Your timing must be exact.

10Your momentum is like the tension of a bent crossbow.
Your timing is like the pulling of a trigger.

War is very complicated and confusing. 4
Battle is chaotic.
Nevertheless, you must not allow chaos.

4War is very sloppy and messy.
Positions turn around.
Nevertheless, you must never be defeated.

7Chaos gives birth to control.
Fear gives birth to courage.
Weakness gives birth to strength.

10You must control chaos.
This depends on your planning.
Your men must brave their fears.
This depends on their momentum.

14You have strengths and weaknesses.
These come from your position.

The concept translated as "timing" is *jie*, which literally means restraint. *Jie* (restraint) is the philosophical counterpart to *shi* (momentum). You hold back force until the right time.

Success requires the overwhelming force created by innovation, and it requires restraint, but "exact timing" in Chinese is literally "brief restraint"—meaning you must control yourself, but not for too long.

The sense here is that the force of momentum and innovation must be held back briefly in order to be released effectively at the right time.

4 The fast-changing environment of martial arts competition is unpredictable. Sun Tzu calls this *juan*, chaos. You plan to use the force of *shi* in order to control the unpredictable *juan* of battle.

No movement in a martial arts contest is ever perfect. Slight errors create openings that can change a match in an instant. You must prepare to protect yourself because you will make mistakes.

The principle that tames the chaos of *juan* is *chi*, control. Your self-control comes from knowing that every situation eventually spawns its opposite condition.

The successful martial artist accepts and even welcomes the confusion of battle. You must leave room in your plans for the unexpected. Martial artists are not threatened by surprising developments. Instead, you use surprise to increase your momentum.

You train in martial arts and study the *Bing-fa* in order to see the strengths and openings in every common situation.

¹⁶You must force the enemy to move to your advantage.

Use your position.

The enemy must follow you.

Surrender a position.

The enemy must take it.

You can offer an advantage to move him.

You can use your men to move him.

You can use your strength to hold him.

You want a successful battle. 5

To do this, you must seek momentum.

Do not just demand a good fight from your people.

You must pick good people and then give them momentum.

⁵You must create momentum.

You create it with your men during battle.

This is comparable to rolling trees and stones.

Trees and stones roll because of their shape and weight.

Offer men safety and they will stay calm.

Endanger them and they will act.

Give them a place and they will hold.

Round them up and they will march.

¹³You make your men powerful in battle with momentum.

This should be like rolling round stones down over a high,

steep cliff.

Momentum is critical.

Once you understand the relative potential of different positions, you can move your opponents to set up an opening. Act as opponents expect you to, and your opponents will react based on their assumptions. Make "mistakes" to give them confidence. They will become convinced that they have an opening. This is how you lure opponents into a weak position. Your efforts can then make their bad situation worse. Once they are at a disadvantage, you can hold them at a disadvantage until they surrender.

5 The goal of meeting opponents is to put them at a disadvantage. You do this with the force of *shi*, created by standard surprises, *jang-qi*. Fighting with others demands working with those who understand these methods and then planning surprises with them.

Shi, or momentum, is a psychological force. You create momentum in a team by understanding human nature. In the confusion of battle, you must understand how people think. People act predictably within limits. People act according to their personality and their self-interest. If nothing changes, people will do what they have done in the past. People will react predictably if you surprise them with danger. People defend positions that they feel are solid. When people are in a group, they follow the example of others.

This lesson ends with an echo of the last verse in the previous chapter. Both chapters teach that good form and momentum empower you. Good positions allow you to take advantage of openings using predictable moves to set up surprises that make you irresistible.

Chapter 6

Weakness and Strength: Go Beyond *Yin* and *Yang*

In studying martial arts, students learn that many aspects of practice are halves of a larger whole. Martial arts are full of *complementary opposites:* defense and attack, inhale and exhale, close and open, soft and hard, fall and raise, slow and fast, recoil and stretch. These opposites are often described as *yin* and *yang.* But *yin* and *yang* —often called the female and male principles—are Taoist ideas. The original complementary opposites in the *Bing-fa* are *xu* and *sat*.

Xu means weak, false, worthless, empty, and hollow. *Sat* is strong, real, wealthy, honest, and solid. The contrasting ideas of *xu* and *sat* rely on each other. *Sat*, strength, is abundance and a temporary state that is the result of action and attaining a new position. *Xu*, weakness, is need and the stable state to which everything returns in the absence of action.

The practice of martial arts creates a sense of circulating internal force (*qi gan*). This sense comes from cycling between complementary opposites: attacking then defending, opening then closing, moving fast then moving slowly. You practice the internal moves (*nei gong*) such as inhaling and exhaling to create this feeling of momentum or force (*qi*). When practicing basic routines such as pushing hands (*tui shou*), you test hardness and softness, that is, emptiness and fullness, to sense the directions of force (*jin lu*) arising from your opponent's movements. On an intellectual level, your movement taking advantage of emptiness or weakness is what creates fullness and strength.

Weakness and Strength

Always arrive first to the empty battlefield to await the 1
enemy at your leisure.
After the battleground is occupied and you hurry to it,
fighting is more difficult.

³You want a successful battle.
Move your men, but not into opposing forces.

⁵You can make the enemy come to you.
Offer him an advantage.
You can make the enemy avoid coming to you.
Threaten him with danger.

⁹When the enemy is fresh, you can tire him.
When he is well fed, you can starve him.
When he is relaxed, you can move him.

Go Beyond *Yin* and *Yang*

THE MARTIAL ARTIST HEARS:

1 *Xu* (weakness, emptiness) and *sat* (strength, fullness) are neither good nor bad. The shift between them creates opportunities. Emptiness is an opening and one kind of opportunity. Strength is a local superiority that creates another kind of opportunity.

Martial arts strategy needs movement toward emptiness to create fullness and movement away from fullness to create emptiness.

You sometimes want your opponents to follow your lead. To get them do that, you must leave an opening into which they can move. You can also keep your opponents from moving into your space. To do that, you must deny them any opening.

The fullness of *sat* also means being rested, well fed, and relaxed. *Bing-fa* teaches that all fullness is temporary. The fullness of an opponent is a condition that you can work or wait to change.

Leave any place without haste. 2
Hurry to where you are unexpected.
You can easily march hundreds of miles without tiring.
To do so, travel through areas that are deserted.
You must take whatever you attack.
Attack when there is no defense.
You must have walls to defend.
Defend where it is impossible to attack.

9Be skilled in attacking.
Give the enemy no idea where to defend.

11Be skillful in your defense.
Give the enemy no idea where to attack.

Be subtle! Be subtle! 3
Arrive without any clear formation.
Ghostly! Ghostly!
Arrive without a sound.
You must use all your skill to control the enemy's decisions.

6Advance where he can't defend.
Charge through his openings.
Withdraw where the enemy cannot chase you.
Move quickly so that he cannot catch you.

2 Martial arts strategy relinquishes defensive positions slowly. However, you must utilize unexpected openings instantly. If you are going in the right direction, you feel energized. Movement through emptiness is quicker and uses less effort than movement into fullness. You move into the emptiness of *xu*, but, since your first responsibility is to defend, you initially seek to block an opponent's moves toward your position. This creates fullness and makes your position impossible to attack.

You continually test your opponents to search out possible openings. Keep them guessing about what you will do next.

You can never take your safety for granted. Discover your own weaknesses before your opponents do.

3 Good fighters never give away their moves before they make them. You must never signal what you intend. Use positions that do not commit you toward any specific action. Make subtle changes in your position that opponents cannot see. Your success comes from controlling the perceptions of others.

You have two choices about how you move toward the emptiness of *xu*. You can attack and move into an opponent's area, but only if your opponent leaves you an opening. You can also elude enemies, moving into emptiness more quickly than they can follow.

[10]Always pick your own battles.
The enemy can hide behind high walls and deep trenches.
Do not try to win by fighting him directly.
Instead, attack a place that he must recapture.
Avoid the battles that you don't want.
You can divide the ground and yet defend it.
Don't give the enemy anything to win.
Divert him by coming to where you defend.

Make other men take a position while you take none. 4
Then focus your forces where the enemy divides his forces.
Where you focus, you unite your forces.
When the enemy divides, he creates many small groups.
You want your large group to attack one of his small ones.
Then you have many men where the enemy has but a few.
Your larger force can overwhelm his smaller one.
Then go on to the next small enemy group.
You can take them one at a time.

You must keep the place that you have chosen as a 5
battleground a secret.
The enemy must not know.
Force the enemy to prepare his defense in many places.
You want the enemy to defend many places.
Then you can choose where to fight.
His forces will be weak there.

In the original Chinese, "battle" is *zhan*, which means "meeting opponents," not necessarily fighting or striking a blow. You assume that your opponents know how to protect themselves against direct attacks. Instead, you look for angles that these opponents are not thinking about. No one can force you to meet an opponent. You define your space in a way that makes it easy to protect. No one should benefit from moving against you. Distract and confuse opponents when they try to get at you.

4 Good fighters are fluid while their opponents take rigid positions. Concentrate on the weaknesses in your opponents' stance. Focus your efforts on one area at a time. Test many areas to break your opponents' concentration on the specific area of weakness you are targeting. Your concentration on specific weaknesses makes rivals easy to beat. When you see them leave an opening there, focus all your strength on the poorly defended area. When they shift their stance to defend that area, move on to another weakness. Each small success adds up to victory over time.

5 You maintain your opponents' ignorance about your real target to make them divide their efforts. If you keep your focus a secret, your opponents must defend many different areas. Without knowing your priorities, your opponents are unable to decide upon their priorities. They must defend against every possible attack. In the *Bing-fa*, the term "fight" means focusing all your efforts in one area. You focus your efforts where your opponent is poorly defended.

7If he reinforces his front lines, he depletes his rear.
If he reinforces his rear, he depletes his front.
If he reinforces his right flank, he depletes his left.
If he reinforces his left flank, he depletes his right.
Without knowing the place of attack, he cannot prepare.
Without knowing the right place, he will be weak everywhere.

13The enemy has weak points.
Prepare your men against them.
He has strong points.
Make his men prepare themselves against you.

You must know the battleground. 6
You must know the time of battle.
You can then travel a thousand miles and still win the battle.

4The enemy should not know the battleground.
He shouldn't know the time of battle.
His left flank will be unable to support his right.
His right will be unable to support his left.
His front lines will be unable to support his rear.
His rear will be unable to support his front.
His support is distant even if it is only ten miles away.
What unknown place can be close?

12You control the balance of forces.
The enemy may have many men but they are superfluous.
How can they help him to victory?

Weak fighters are always shifting their focus. They are easily distracted by every passing potential threat or opposing move. They jump from one position to another. The result is that they are always out of balance. Weak fighters never identify their real weaknesses so they don't know where they must focus their attention. Without having a focus, they are weak everywhere.

The choices you make are ultimately simple. You focus your efforts on areas of weakness and emptiness. You don't let opponents know where you are focusing so that they cannot counteract your efforts in time to be effective against you.

6 The position you fight from (ground—*di*) and changing conditions (climate—*tian*) define the place and time of battle. No work is wasted if it gets you to the right position and time.

Pick styles and movements with which your opponents are unfamiliar. Pick the moment to attack in which your opponents are unprepared. When people are unfamiliar with a style, they cannot be certain of how to react appropriately. When people are uncertain, they react emotionally. When contests fail to go as planned, people begin thinking about their situation. When people are busy thinking, they are easily taken by surprise. Surprise makes it impossible to respond well. Ignorance makes every response difficult.

You alone must know when and where you are ready to attack. Pick a point at which your opponents' strengths are neutralized. Size and strength are unimportant in achieving success.

¹⁵We say:
You must let victory happen.

¹⁷The enemy may have many men.
You can still control him without a fight.

When you form your strategy, know the strengths and 7
weaknesses of your plan.
When you execute a plan, know how to manage both action
and inaction.
When you take a position, know the deadly and the winning
grounds.
When you enter into battle, know when you have too many
or too few men.

⁵Use your position as your war's centerpiece.
Arrive at the battle without a formation.
Don't take a position in advance.
Then even the best spies can't report it.
Even the wisest general cannot plan to counter you.
Take a position where you can triumph using superior numbers.
Keep opposing forces ignorant.
Everyone should learn your location after your position has
given you success.
No one should know how your location gives you a winning
position.
Make a successful battle one from which the enemy cannot
recover.
You must continually adjust your position to his position.

You must be opportunistic. You must take what opponents give you and accept what you are given.

Emptiness and fullness, wholeness and division, and place and time give you the necessary momentary advantage.

7 The principles of *xu sat* (emptiness/fullness) affect every step in a contest. Your knowledge of *xu sat* exposes your own strengths and weaknesses. During a contest, *xu sat* tells you when to move (*hang*) and when to stay where you are. When you concentrate your forces at a position (*xing*), *xu sat* allows you to pick the right place and time. Your opponent's ignorance of that place and time determines the relative balance of force and power. You must choose contacts that are best suited to your capabilities.

Your success depends on working opponents out of position. Your position should enable you to focus your efforts and strengths at a specific point at a specific time. This cannot be attempted before your opponents leave an opening because it gives them the knowledge from which they can create the appropriate defense to counter your move. You need a superior focus at the point of attack. You can only achieve that superior force if your opponents are ignorant about where to defend. They should think about their weakness there only after you have struck against it. If your opponents cannot guess what you intend, they cannot move to fill the openings that you see. Executed correctly, this makes you so powerful at the chosen place and time that your concentration of force is impossible to counter and certain of success. Opponents cannot react quickly enough to undermine your efforts because they are out of position.

Manage your military formations like water. 8
Water takes every shape.
It avoids the high and moves to the low.
Your war can take any shape.
It must avoid the strong and strike the weak.
Water follows the shape of the land that directs its flow.
Your forces follow the enemy, who determines how you win.

[8]Make war without a standard approach.
Water has no consistent shape.
If you follow the enemy's shifts and changes, you can always
find a way to win.
We call this shadowing.

[12]Fight five different campaigns without a firm rule for victory.
Use all four seasons without a consistent position.
Your timing must be sudden.
A few weeks determine your failure or success.

8 Water is Sun Tzu's analogy for change. It is the classical Chinese element associated by the *Bing-fa* with the changing climate. The flow of water toward emptiness reflects the nature of opportunism. Every competitive contest is different. You must always change your approach to focus your strengths on an opponent's weaknesses. Your opponent's choice of form or position is the basis (ground) of his or her weaknesses. You must react to that choice. Opponents' decisions create the openings you seek.

Water also symbolizes changing your martial arts methods. In contests, you cannot always repeat the same moves that you have already used. Your opponents are learning. You must react to your opponents without making your moves predictable.

Water is the element of *tian*—heaven, another word for climate. Changes in trends generate new opportunities. You react quickly to those opportunities before your window of opportunity closes. Your success or failure is determined by how you use your time.

Chapter 7

Armed Conflict: Understand Real Fights

Sun Tzu makes it clear that real conflict (*zheng*) is not the most desirable path to success. The martial arts are different from other sports in that they are designed for self-defense. The most successful martial artists are those who others are afraid to challenge. You prepare for real fights with real bad guys, but your goal is always to avoid them. The *Bing-fa* warns against engaging in real battles without a decisive advantage.

Sun Tzu begins this chapter by explaining that tests of strength are best avoided. Your real opportunities lie in taking your own path, distancing yourself from the crowd, avoiding confrontations. The focus of martial arts strategy is learning and self-mastery, not beating others. You make the best progress through training and contests, not fighting real battles. Real battles can only slow you down, especially if you are injured.

You cannot force favorable showdowns with real bad guys. When you obviously will win, bad guys will avoid you. You can win confrontations that cannot be avoided by lulling opponents into a false sense of security. Communication is often the key. Martial artists always speak humbly, both to avoid confrontations and tp lull real-world bad guys into overconfidence.

Martial artists choose the right time and place for unavoidable confrontations. You must be patient enough to wait until everything is in your favor. You must also remember that your real goal is to remove an obstacle, not to prove your skill.

Armed Conflict

SUN TZU SAID:

Everyone uses the arts of war. 1
You accept orders from the government.
Then you assemble your army.
You organize your men and build camps.
You must avoid disasters from armed conflict.

⁶Seeking armed conflict can be disastrous.
Because of this, a detour can be the shortest path.
Because of this, problems can become opportunities.

⁹Use an indirect route as your highway.
Use the search for advantage to guide you.
When you fall behind, you must catch up.
When you get ahead, you must wait.
You must know the detour that most directly accomplishes
your plan.

¹⁴Undertake armed conflict when you have an advantage.
Seeking armed conflict for its own sake is dangerous.

Understand Real Fights

THE MARTIAL ARTIST HEARS:

1 Everyone, even those who are not trained in the martial arts or the *Bing-fa*, tries to think strategically. Everyone has personal desires. Everyone has his or her own resources. Everyone organizes his or her priorities and chooses a position. Everyone is also trying to avoid real-world fights that are destructive even if they are won.

Martial force (*bing*) does not seek real conflict (*zheng*). The martial arts require learning to win by avoiding real fights. This is how weaknesses are turned into strengths rather than injuries.

Instead of looking for conflict, you look for opportunities by moving (*hang*), using "detours." As less traveled paths, detours are a form of emptiness (*xu*) and offer the possibility of advancing your position easily. Getting ahead of yourself is what is truly dangerous. You make faster progress if you can find ways to avoid the real opponents that stand in your path.

You only fight real battles when you are certain to gain something valuable. Every fight that cannot be avoided is inherently risky.

You can build up an army to fight for an advantage. 2
Then you won't catch the enemy.
You can force your army to go fight for an advantage.
Then you abandon your heavy supply wagons.

5You keep only your armor and hurry after the enemy.
You avoid stopping day or night.
You use many roads at the same time.
You go hundreds of miles to fight for an advantage.
Then the enemy catches your commanders and your army.
Your strong soldiers get there first.
Your weaker soldiers follow behind.
Using this approach, only one in ten will arrive.
You can try to go fifty miles to fight for an advantage.
Then your commanders and army will stumble.
Using this method, only half of your soldiers will make it.
You can try to go thirty miles to fight for an advantage.
Then only two out of three will get there.

18If you make your army travel without good supply lines,
your army will die.
Without supplies and food, your army will die.
If you don't save the harvest, your army will die.

2 Good fighters do not attempt to force decisive showdowns with real-world enemies. Your opponents can easily avoid these situations. It is always a mistake to chase after confrontation. Your impatience undermines any support you get from others.

No skill in defense can protect you from arrogance and impatience. Impatience is dangerous because it wearies you. Arrogance is dangerous because it encourages attempting more than you can accomplish. Impatience for a showdown tempts you to overextend yourself. When you are overextended, you are likely to make bad choices and waste your limited supply of internal resources. You may start off strong. However, you will finish poorly. Nine times out of ten, going out of your way to look for a showdown leads to overextending yourself and failure. Arrogantly looking for a showdown puts you off balance. Then you are more inclined to make mistakes. Being off balance always depletes your resources. Putting yourself on enemy ground looking for a showdown takes you out of position. Being out of position always weakens you.

Martial artists don't look for real-world fights because fighting will undermine their long-term support from others. Martial artists don't look for fights that strain their resources. Martial artists don't look for fights that cannot benefit them.

[21]Do not let any of your potential enemies know what you
are planning.
Still, you must not hesitate to form alliances.
You must know the mountains and forests.
You must know where the obstructions are.
You must know where the marshes are.
If you don't, you cannot move the army.
If you don't, you must use local guides.
If you don't, you can't take advantage of the terrain.

You make war by making a false stand. 3
By finding an advantage, you can move.
By dividing and joining, you can reinvent yourself and trans-
form the situation.
You can move as quickly as the wind.
You can rise like the forest.
You can invade and plunder like fire.
You can stay as motionless as a mountain.
You can be as mysterious as the fog.
You can strike like sounding thunder.

[10]Divide your troops to plunder the villages.
When on open ground, dividing is an advantage.
Don't worry about organization; just move.
Be the first to find a new route that leads directly to a win-
ning plan.
This is how you are successful at armed conflict.

Instead of looking for confrontations, you must move based upon your desire to avoid real-world confrontations. Rather than chasing after fights, you should keep potentially dangerous opponents in the dark about your intentions. Instead of seeking conflict, you should seek alliances. All movement must be based on knowledge of the ground. The most basic principle of the *Bing-fa* is that knowledge of the ground makes good positioning (*xing*) possible. Good positioning, not conflict, is the source of real advantage or opportunity.

3 You must not let potentially dangerous people think that you are against them. Your best opportunity to move forward is avoiding them entirely. If you cannot avoid them, your goal should be to make them think that you are willing to be friendly with them. You can then get away from them as quickly as possible. You can learn their strengths and weaknesses. You need to know how dangerous people might hamper your progress. You need to learn where you might get trapped. Without creating a challenge, you must appear unmovable. Let dangerous people know as little as possible about you. You can then surprise them by defending yourself if necessary.

Making yourself seem less successful than you are protects your resources. In situations in which you might be challenged, appearing weak is an advantage. Don't worry about what others think; focus on your own progress. Be creative about finding an easy way around the dangerous people who might confront you. Outmaneuvering opponents is how you are successful in real-world fights.

Martial experience says: 4
"You can speak, but you will not be heard.
You must use gongs and drums.
You cannot really see your forces just by looking.
You must use banners and flags."

⁶You must master gongs, drums, banners, and flags.
Place people as a single unit where they can all see and hear.
You must unite them as one.
Then the brave cannot advance alone.
The fearful cannot withdraw alone.
You must force them to act as a group.

¹²In night battles, you must use numerous fires and drums.
In day battles, you must use many banners and flags.
You must position your people to control what they see and
hear.

You control your army by controlling its morale. 5
As a general, you must be able to control emotions.

³In the morning, a person's energy is high.
During the day, it fades.
By evening, a person's thoughts turn to home.
You must use your troops wisely.
Avoid the enemy's high spirits.
Strike when his men are lazy and want to go home.
This is how you master energy.

4 At this point, the topic changes from avoiding real-world battles to winning in fights when you can't avoid them. The first key to winning a real fight is making a lot of noise. You must work hard to get the attention of those around you. You can get aid from unexpected areas if you make your situation clear.

Communication is how you control confrontations. You must control what others, both your opponents and potential allies, see and hear. You need to get other people on your side. If you are too aggressive, you alienate others and increase the hostility against you. If you are too timid, you lose the support of others and invite attacks. You must offer a reason for others to join with you.

When it is night, you must make more noise. During the day, you use motion to signal others. You must expect others to interpret their situation, whether it is safe to attack you or join you, based upon what they see and hear you do.

5 After good communication, the second most important key in confrontation is controlling your and your opponents' emotions.

The first technique of controlling emotional energy (*hei*) is largely a matter of using the correct timing. Conserve your energy before a confrontation. You must avoid tiring yourself. Force an unavoidable confrontation when your opponent wants it least. Husband your energy. Opponents fight more adamantly when they are fresh. If you wait until later when they are tired, they will want to back down. Match your vigor against an opponent's weariness.

10Use discipline to await the chaos of battle.
Keep relaxed to await a crisis.
This is how you master emotion.

13Stay close to home to await the distant enemy.
Stay comfortable to await the weary enemy.
Stay well fed to await the hungry enemy.
This is how you master power.

Don't entice the enemy when his ranks are orderly. 6
You must not attack when his formations are solid.
This is how you master adaptation.

4You must follow these martial rules.
Do not take a position facing the high ground.
Do not oppose those with their backs to the wall.
Do not follow those who pretend to flee.
Do not attack the enemy's strongest men.
Do not swallow the enemy's bait.
Do not block an army that is heading home.
Leave an escape outlet for a surrounded army.
Do not press a desperate foe.
This is how you use martial skills.

The next technique for winning in conflict is control, meaning self-discipline and self-control. In the *Bing-fa*, self-control means using patience and waiting while controlling your emotions.

Finally, plan unavoidable real-world fights in a place that favors you. Plan them at a time of day that favors you. Plan confrontations when your opponents have other issues to deal with. "Power" here is the Chinese concept of *lei*, which means "quality" or "merit."

6 A true master of martial arts avoids the mistake of overconfidence. You must avoid real-world battles with well-prepared opponents. Your success depends only upon your flexibility.

You must let your situation dictate your decisions. Never fight in a position that faces natural forces such as gravity or the wind. You must always leave your opponents a way to save face to end the fights, but you must avoid the temptation to overextend yourself. You must aim only at your opponents' weakest points. Expect those you are fighting to try to deceive and trick you. Allow your opponents an easy way to back down. Make it easy for them to claim victory when they decide that you are not worth fighting. Don't force them into fighting for their lives. Desperation makes any opponent more dangerous.

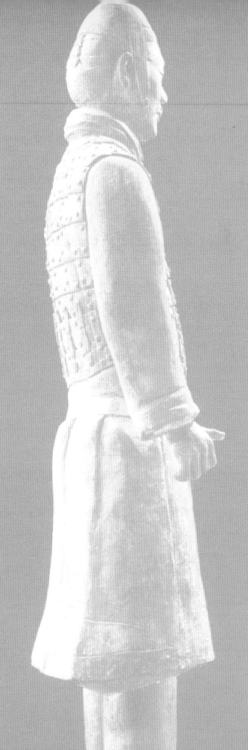

Chapter 8

Adaptability: Adjust to Conditions

The Chinese name for this chapter means literally "many changes." The concept of change, or *bian,* in the *Bing-fa* includes both our efforts to change a situation and our reaction to changing conditions. Martial arts strategy requires continually adjusting to change. Regular people pay very little attention to what is happening around them and tend to react in the same ways regardless of their situation. Successful strategy is dynamic and based on the willingness, even eagerness, to adjust to changes.

This chapter serves as an introduction to the next three chapters. These chapters describe specific situations, how to recognize their conditions, and how to respond appropriately to them. Martial arts training teaches you to recognize these situations as opportunities and to know how to take advantage of them.

Good fighters make a habit of change while poor fighters are unable to change their habits. Though it seems counterintuitive, you must change to be consistent because consistency requires continually adapting to changing situations. In dealing with change, the best defense is a good offense. If you don't leverage the opportunities of a changing world, others will almost certainly use those changes against you.

The biggest risk in adjusting to change comes from overreacting. The *Bing-fa* teaches that your strengths can become dangerous when they are taken to extremes. During a battle, the increased pace of change pressures you toward those extremes.

Adaptability

SUN TZU SAID:

Everyone uses the arts of war. 1
As a general, you get your orders from the government.
You gather your troops.
On dangerous ground, you must not camp.
Where the roads intersect, you must join your allies.
When an area is cut off, you must not delay in it.
When you are surrounded, you must scheme.
In a life-or-death situation, you must fight.
There are roads that you must not take.
There are armies that you must not fight.
There are strongholds that you must not attack.
There are positions that you must not defend.
There are government commands that must not be obeyed.

14Military leaders must be experts in knowing how to adapt
to find an advantage.
This will teach you the use of war.

16Some commanders are not good at making adjustments to
find an advantage.
They can know the shape of the terrain.
Still, they cannot find an advantageous position.

Adjust to Conditions

1 The list of situations and reactions given here is a sampling of the many such situations detailed in the next three chapters. Each teaches that you must be responsive to your situation. You must respect those in authority over you. In risky situations, you cannot pretend you are safe. When the risks are shared, you cannot act as though you are alone. When you face overwhelming odds, you can still find an opening. Fighting, that is, using all your resources, is necessary only when you run out of options. You must know where your decisions lead. You must avoid making enemies of the wrong people. You must avoid attacking an opponent's strengths. You must always change your thinking rather than fight to defend bad decisions. Know when doing what you have been told will be a mistake.

The Chinese term *tong* means "expert." It also means "open" and "to move unobstructed." A martial arts expert is, by definition, open to new ways, without any mental barriers to moving a new way.

When fighters lack *tong*, they are closed to new opportunities and hamstrung by their plans. They can see their situation—the lay of the land—but they are handicapped by their narrow viewpoints. They are not open to the possibility of finding a better response.

[19]Some military commanders do not know how to adjust
their methods.
They can find an advantageous position.
Still, they cannot use their men effectively.

You must be creative in your planning. 2
You must adapt to your opportunities and weaknesses.
You can use a variety of approaches and still have a consis-
tent result.
You must adjust to a variety of problems and consistently
solve them.

You can deter your potential enemy by using his 3
weaknesses against him.
You can keep your potential enemy's army busy by giving it
work to do.
You can rush your potential enemy by offering him an
advantageous position.

You must make use of war. 4
Do not trust that the enemy isn't coming.
Trust your readiness to meet him.
Do not trust that the enemy won't attack.
Rely only on your ability to pick a place that the enemy can't
attack.

Zhi is the knowledge and skills gained by listening to others. When fighters lack *zhi*, they can still have the *tong*, or openness, to recognize opportunities. Their weakness is that they lack the knowledge of how to respond, so they cannot use their strengths properly.

2 Martial arts strategy teaches you not to be rigid in your planning. In strategy, plans are constantly adapted to the ever-shifting flows of *xu* and *sat*. Your goal must be consistent results, but you must adjust your responses to the situation to achieve that goal. In competitive situations, consistent actions never yield consistent results because your opponents constantly adjust to your responses.

3 Good fighters know how to take the initiative to prevent others from stopping them. Rather than responding to your opponents' moves, you must force them to react to your moves. To do this, you must understand their weaknesses and make them work to defend their weaknesses. You can rush your opponents into making mistakes by offering them openings that close quickly.

4 Skill in adaptability means that you are always prepared for the worst. Strategy demands that you assume that your competition is every bit as capable as you are. As the situation changes, you must assume that your opponent knows how to take advantage of it. The secret is that success starts with survival. This means that you must always be looking for ways in which opponents can attack you.

You can exploit five different faults in a leader. 5
If he is willing to die, you can kill him.
If he wants to survive, you can capture him.
He may have a quick temper.
You can then provoke him with insults.
If he has a delicate sense of honor, you can disgrace him.
If he loves his people, you can create problems for him.
In every situation, look for these five weaknesses.
They are common faults in commanders.
They always lead to military disaster.

[11]To overturn an army, you must kill its general.
To do this, you must use these five weaknesses.
You must always look for them.

In the first chapter, the *Bing-fa* said that good strategists must be brave, smart, caring, strict, and trusting. Bravery is good, but too much courage is foolhardy. Intelligence is good, but too much analysis leads to paralysis. Caring is good, but too much caring becomes a trigger to emotional, rather than strategic, responses. Discipline sets high standards, but perfectionists are easily frustrated. Trusting people is a good thing, but it is dangerous to become dependent on people. Neither you nor your opponents are perfect. An opponent's weakness is your opportunity. Your weakness is an opponent's opportunity.

Martial arts are less a physical battle than a mental one. Adaptability is primarily a decision-making skill. People's character flaws directly affect the type of adjustments they can make.

♦ ♦ ♦

Chapter 9

Armed March: Maintain Forward Progress

Making forward progress changes your situation. In this chapter, the *Bing-fa* teaches the skills you will need to make progress in the face of that opposition. Martial artists know that the key to overcoming opposition is choosing the appropriate response. Choosing the appropriate response depends on correctly diagnosing the situation. This requires knowing what the science of strategy teaches about the right response.

Sun Tzu categorizes situations by their unevenness (inequality), pace of change (dynamics), and uncertainty. These different conditions demand different responses. A fighter cannot simply do as he or she pleases. A good fighter only does what the situation requires. As you move forward, you must be aware of how your situation changes, and you must be properly positioned to meet opponents.

Principles and ethics are critical to strong positioning. Competition does not take place in a social vacuum. You need people to support you. Few people are willing to support those without ethics.

Progress requires embracing change, but change creates problems. Change also creates openings for others to attack you. You must know how to be cautious when you are making good progress.

To outmaneuver your opponents, you need to understand what they are doing. Good fighters know that actions speak louder than words. Opponents never do anything without a purpose. Learning strategy means understanding what motivates people. You want to use that motivation to rally people to support you.

Armed March

SUN TZU SAID:

Anyone moving an army must adjust to the enemy. 1
When caught in the mountains, rely on their valleys.
Position yourself on the heights facing the sun.
To win your battles, never attack uphill.
This is how you position your army in the mountains.

6When water blocks you, keep far away from it.
Let the invader cross the river and wait for him.
Do not meet him in midstream.
Wait for him to get half his forces across and then take
advantage of the situation.

10You need to be able to fight.
You can't do that if you are caught in water when you meet
an invader.
Position yourself upstream, facing the sun.
Never face against the current.
Always position your army upstream when near the water.

Maintain Forward Progress

THE MARTIAL ARTIST HEARS:

1 Maintaining forward progress requires knowing how to use different types of ground against opponents as you move forward. When the ground is uneven, follow the path of least resistance. You use the unevenness of the ground by never meeting opponents when they control the high ground.

Water is the *Bing-fa*'s metaphor for change (*bian*). When a change in the environment becomes an obstacle, you must be cautious. If others are tempted into making difficult transitions, you must be patient. You should never join them. You want to meet your opponents when they are in the middle of negotiating a transition.

You must focus on using all your resources against your opponents. This means you cannot waste resources fighting the environment you are in. You cannot battle the wind, the currents, and gravity and deal with your opponents at the same time. You must use the pressure of the forces in your favor. Use temporary changes in climate the same way that you use changes in ground in uneven areas.

¹⁵You may have to move across marshes.
Move through them quickly without stopping.
You may meet the enemy in the middle of a marsh.
You must keep on the water grasses.
Keep your back to a clump of trees.
This is how you position your army in a marsh.

²¹On a level plateau, take a position that you can change.
Keep the higher ground on your right and to the rear.
Keep danger in front of you and safety behind.
This is how you position yourself on a level plateau.

²⁵You can find an advantage in all four of these situations.
Learn from the great emperor who used positioning to
conquer his four rivals.

Armies are stronger on high ground and weaker on low. **2**
They are better camping on sunny southern hillsides than
on shady northern ones.
Provide for your army's health and place men correctly.
Your army will be free from disease.
Done correctly, this means victory.

⁶You must sometimes defend on a hill or riverbank.
You must keep on the south side in the sun.
Keep the uphill slope at your right rear.

⁹This will give the advantage to your army.
It will always give you a position of strength.

Marshes are the *Bing-fa*'s metaphor for areas where the ground is uncertain and unpredictable. You must move through these areas quickly without getting bogged down. Opponents will move against you when they think your footing is uncertain. Pay attention to your immediate surroundings to identify islands of stability. You must protect your back to prevent getting pushed into worse trouble.

The ideal ground is level, stable, and solid. However, no playing field is perfect and you can use even slight advantages in your favor. Your position must focus on your opponents, facing them directly, but maintaining a fallback position.

No matter what the conditions are on the ground, you should think about the opportunities it offers, not its problems. You must learn to master the techniques to meet opponents under any conditions.

2 This discussion of mountains translates height into a metaphor for the ethical "high ground." In the *Bing-fa*, the terms *yin* and *yang* refer specifically to shady and sunny hillsides (not female and male), but they are metaphors for hidden and visible positions. Honorable positions are open to scrutiny. Corrupt positions are shady. Ethical positions create healthy groups. Shady positions do not.

Sometimes you are forced to defend a questionable position. You can still be honest about your situation and see clearly where you stand. The idea is to always keep natural forces on your side.

Over the millennia, people have seen that strong principles create opportunities. Principles create unity, the source of strength.

Stop the march when the rain swells the river into rapids. 3
You may want to ford the river.
Wait until it subsides.

⁴All regions can have seasonal mountain streams that can
cut you off.
There are seasonal lakes.
There are seasonal blockages.
There are seasonal jungles.
There are seasonal floods.
There are seasonal fissures.
Get away from all these quickly.
Do not get close to them.
Keep them at a distance.
Maneuver the enemy close to them.
Position yourself facing these dangers.
Push the enemy back into them.

¹⁶Danger can hide on your army's flank.
There are reservoirs and lakes.
There are reeds and thickets.
There are mountain woods.
Their dense vegetation provides a hiding place.
You must cautiously search through them.
They can always hide an ambush.

3 This discussion of water focuses on change in climate. Challenging periods of change can affect your position at any time. When the climate shifts, you must patiently hold your position.

The element of climate focuses on changes over time. Time continually reshapes your situation, creating new potential obstacles. In the *Bing-fa*, you see the natural process as shifting between extremes. What was once dry ground becomes a lake. What was once a lake becomes dry ground. These changes can stop you. Other changes are confusing. Some changes can be suddenly overwhelming. Some problems seem to be bottomless pits.

Martial arts strategy treats change as both a danger and an opportunity. Speed avoids its dangers so the sooner you react to change the better. It is always better to avoid temporary obstacles than to deal with them. You can use your opponents' ignorance of changes against them. An opponent's first instinct is to oppose you. You can use this reaction to pin him or her against new obstacles.

Movement creates change. It brings you onto new ground where not all dangers are readily apparent. The environment can hide potential threats and dangers. Again, this is both a problem and an opportunity. Good strategy is based on knowledge of the ground. A lack of knowledge is a cause for investigation. You can use the ground to hide your position and movement. You must be suspicious when opponents can hide their positions and movements.

Sometimes, the enemy is close by but remains calm. 4
Expect to find him in a natural stronghold.
Other times he remains at a distance but provokes battle.
He wants you to attack him.

5He sometimes shifts the position of his camp.
He is looking for an advantageous position.

7The trees in the forest move.
Expect that the enemy is coming.
The tall grasses obstruct your view.
Be suspicious.

11The birds take flight.
Expect that the enemy is hiding.
Animals startle.
Expect an ambush.

15Notice the dust.
It sometimes rises high in a straight line.
Vehicles are coming.
The dust appears low in a wide band.
Foot soldiers are coming.
The dust seems scattered in different areas.
The enemy is collecting firewood.
Any dust is light and settling down.
The enemy is setting up camp.

4 This section covers "marshes," that is, uncertain ground, but the metaphor is broadened to focus on interpreting the condition of opponents, which is always uncertain. For example, when they are confident and want you to attack, they have a secret advantage.

When opponents change their approach, it means that they've seen a hidden opportunity or discovered a secret weakness.

You often cannot see your opposition's moves directly, but you can infer them from what you see in the larger environment and from what you learn from others in the area. If you can't get good information from these sources, you must be suspicious.

You can know when the opposition is planning to surprise you by curious changes in the behavior of others. If someone knows the secret plans of your opponents, he or she will act nervously and overreact for no apparent reason.

"Dust" (*chen*) is a Chinese character showing deer kicking up dirt. As such, it represents the fundamental idea that nothing can move in the environment without leaving signs. Everything you do kicks up dirt, leaving signals that others can interpret. You can know an opponent's movements by carefully evaluating the smallest hints. Without knowing specifics, you can get an idea of your opponents' actions by the amount of evidence of activity you find, the pattern of evidence, and by its increase or decrease. You have to continually monitor even the smallest rumors about competitive activity to put together a meaningful picture of this activity.

Your enemy speaks humbly while building up forces. **5**
He is planning to advance.

³The enemy talks aggressively and pushes as if to advance.
He is planning to retreat.

⁵Small vehicles exit his camp first.
They move the army's flanks.
They are forming a battle line.

⁸Your enemy tries to sue for peace but without offering a
treaty.
He is plotting.

¹⁰Your enemy's men run to leave and yet form ranks.
You should expect action.

¹²Half his army advances and the other half retreats.
He is luring you.

¹⁴Your enemy plans to fight but his men just stand there.
They are starving.

¹⁶Those who draw water drink it first.
They are thirsty.

¹⁸Your enemy sees an advantage but does not advance.
His men are tired.

5 This section covers the "plateau" where the ground is equal so opponents use deception and alliances to improve their position.

For this reason, you shouldn't fear aggressive behavior; it is often a smoke screen for weakness. Worry instead about feigned weakness.

Since you usually want to avoid direct tests of strength, you should be sensitive to any indication that your opponents are planning to put up a fight. You should never fight on an opponent's terms.

However, this doesn't mean that you should trust opponents who want to call a truce, especially without being specific why. You want to avoid confrontations, but you must distrust false offers.

You must also expect that opponents will try to mislead you with actions as well as words, feigning one move while planning another.

You must suspect what looks like obvious confusion on the part of your opponents. This is a subtler form of feint.

You can more honestly judge your opponents' condition by their associates' behavior. People often misjudge their associates' abilities.

People act in their individual self-interest. If an opponent has allies, you can expect those allies to act in their own self-interest.

If an opponent fails to seize an obvious opportunity, it is only because he truly lacks the resources to do so.

²⁰Birds gather.
Your enemy has abandoned his camp.

²²Your enemy's soldiers call in the night.
They are afraid.

²⁴Your enemy's army is raucous.
The men do not take their commander seriously.

²⁶Your enemy's banners and flags shift.
Order is breaking down.

²⁸Your enemy's officers are irritable.
They are exhausted.

³⁰Your enemy's men kill their horses for meat.
They are out of provisions.

³²They don't put their pots away or return to their tents.
They are desperate.

³⁴Enemy troops appear sincere and agreeable.
But their men are slow to speak to each other.
They are no longer united.

³⁷Your enemy offers too many incentives to his men.
He is in trouble.

³⁹Your enemy gives out too many punishments.
His men are weary.

When an opponent abandons an established position, it creates activity in the environment as others move into that position.

When a group of opponents show their emotions, their fear is contagious, affecting the whole group.

Any group of fighters can lose control of itself. This happens only when they are not guided by a trusted leader.

Reorganization is another sign of internal friction, fractures, and the breakdown of unity and focus in a group.

When opponents get angry, they make poor decisions, which is dangerous, but weariness is the source of most anger.

Only desperate opponents give up their ability to move. Only survival is more important.

When your opponents are really in bad shape, however, they can become more dangerous.

Communication is the key to coordination in any group. People can claim that they are working with others, but if they fail to share information, the group is divided.

Opponents shouldn't have to bribe their supporters to join them. This is a sign of weakness.

Opponents also shouldn't have to overdiscipline or punish their supporters. This is another sign of weakness.

⁴¹Your enemy first acts violently and then is afraid of your
larger force.

His best troops have not arrived.

⁴³Your enemy comes in a conciliatory manner.

He needs to rest and recuperate.

⁴⁵Your enemy is angry and appears to welcome battle.

This goes on for a long time, but he doesn't attack.

He also doesn't leave the field.

You must watch him carefully.

If you are too weak to fight, you must find more men. 6

In this situation, you must not act aggressively.

You must unite your forces.

Prepare for the enemy.

Recruit men and stay where you are.

⁶You must be cautious about making plans and adjust to the
enemy.

You must gather more men.

Speed is a critical factor in competition. This means that your opponents may sometimes attack before they are truly ready, as a stalling tactic to throw you off balance and delay your advance.

If opponents can use a confrontation as a delaying tactic, they can also pretend to make peace as a delaying tactic as well.

Sometimes opponents' behavior is just confusing. Do they want a direct confrontation or not? In these cases, the *Bing-fa* advises that you avoid initiating any action. You must wait and see what the competition does.

6 All forms of forward progress have their natural limits. When you move forward, you have to know when to stop. At some point, your resources are stretched too thin to continue advancing. You must then stop and assume a defensive posture. For a group, this means recruiting new members.

When you are regrouping your forces, avoid thinking about openings and just focus on what your opponents are doing. You must buy time to build up your resources.

With new, undedicated soldiers, you can depend on them 7
if you discipline them.
They will tend to disobey your orders.
If they do not obey your orders, they will be useless.

4You can depend on seasoned, dedicated soldiers.
But you must avoid disciplining them without reason.
Otherwise, you cannot use them.

7You must control your soldiers with esprit de corps.
You must bring them together by winning victories.
You must get them to believe in you.

10Make it easy for people to know what to do by training
your people.
Your people will then obey you.
If you do not make it easy for people to know what to do,
you won't train your people.
Then they will not obey.

14Make your commands easy to follow.
You must understand the way a crowd thinks.

✦ ✦ ✦

7 When you bring new people onto a group, you must be very clear about their responsibilities and strict in enforcing rules. By demanding a lot from your new people, you make it clear up front that you are going to challenge them to live up to your standards.

You must take a very different approach in managing your seasoned partners. As tough as you are on new people, you must give your proven allies a great deal of respect.

People want to identify themselves with a winner. People truly become an integral part of a group when they play a role in its success. Success in the past builds confidence in the future.

Training people means giving them knowledge. This starts with understanding the students' shared purpose or philosophy, the source of the group's unity and focus. However, it also means clearly training them in their specific roles and procedures, the realm of methods. The more clearly you define roles and responsibilities, the better people work in a group.

Martial arts strategy teaches you that simplicity is the key to creating a winning group psychology.

Chapter 10

地 形

Field Position: Conform to the Ground

This chapter examines six characteristics that you use to evaluate both the ground around you and your own form. In martial arts strategy, positioning or form includes all aspects of focusing your resources at a specific place and time in a competitive contest.

Field position, that is, the shape of the ground and your position on it, determines the future potential of your efforts. A given field position or form—literally "ground form" (*di xing*)—is evaluated based on its potential for assisting a move forward or defending yourself. Each field position acts as a stepping-stone to a future position, but to use a field position correctly you must understand how a position's nature dictates your future options.

Good fighters know how to make the right moves so that each step makes the step after that easier. Martial arts strategy provides a method for weighing your opportunities so you can make the right choices. After a while, you will instantly see where each choice naturally leads.

Martial artists do not make choices to satisfy other people's expectations. You are the only person in a position to choose the right course. You cannot make choices based upon a desire to win praise or avoid criticism. The ethics of martial arts requires that you act as a leader and role model. Giving people what they need is more important than giving them what they want. Choosing the right path in life is a matter of being objective about your obstacles and capabilities while holding to your principles.

Field Position

Some field positions are unobstructed. 1
Some field positions are entangling.
Some field positions are supporting.
Some field positions are constricted.
Some field positions give you a barricade.
Some field positions are spread out.

7You can attack from some positions easily.
Other forces can meet you easily as well.
You call these unobstructed positions.
These positions are open.
In them, be the first to occupy a high, sunny area.
Put yourself where you can defend your supply routes.
Then you will have an advantage.

Conform to the Ground

THE MARTIAL ARTIST HEARS:

1 The *Bing-fa* offers six extreme forms of ground. "Unobstructed" is *tong*, the idea of openness. It also means "expert." "Entangling" is *gua*, literally meaning "to hang." Its opposite is "supporting," *zhii*, meaning "to prop up." "Constricted," *ai*, means "narrow." "Barricaded," *xian*, means "obstructed," the opposite of *tong*, open. "Spread out" is *yuan*, meaning "far," opposite of *ai*, constricted.

These six forms are the two extremes of three dimensions. The first dimension is "obstacles," *xian*. This dimension ranges from the barricaded position, *xian*, to the unobstructed position, *tong*. Unobstructed ground allows you to move on easily, but it is open to attack. Unobstructed ground forms offer an advantage for movement—specifically attack—but they are bad for defense. They are good but temporary stepping-stones to stronger positions.

¹⁴You can attack from some positions easily.
Disaster arises when you try to return to them.
These are entangling positions.
These field positions are one-sided.
Wait until your enemy is unprepared.
You can then attack from these positions and win.
Avoid a well-prepared enemy.
You will try to attack and lose.
Since you can't return, you will meet disaster.
These field positions offer no advantage.

²⁴You cannot leave some positions without losing an advantage.
If the enemy leaves this ground, he also loses an advantage.
You call these supporting field positions.
These positions strengthen you.
The enemy may try to entice you away.
Still, hold your position.
You must entice the enemy to leave.
You then strike him as he is leaving.
These field positions offer an advantage.

³³Some field positions are constricted.
Get to these positions first.
You must fill these areas and await the enemy.
Sometimes, the enemy will reach them first.
If he fills them, do not follow him.
However, if he fails to fill them, you can go after him.

The next dimension is a stickiness that the *Bing-fa* calls *ee*, which is translated as "danger," but which also means "adversity" or "opposition." Its first extreme is *gua*, entangling ground. You can attack from an entangling position, but you cannot return to positions on this ground. It is dangerous because it doesn't leave you a fallback position if your attack is unsuccessful. It is like a one-way street. You must be patient to use these positions. You must be certain your next move is solid. Do not move out of these positions unless you are certain. This ground offers you no fallback position. Moving onto this ground is a false opportunity.

The other extreme of *ee*, the danger dimension, is the supporting position, which is dangerous only if you try to leave it. You get stuck on entangling ground because you can't return, but you get stuck on supporting ground because you cannot abandon it. Think of a hilltop. It is easy to move away off a hilltop because every direction is down, but if you follow the path of least resistance, you get weaker with each step. You cannot take these positions for granted. If opponents are on supporting ground, you cannot attack them. If an opponent abandons one of these positions, you should attack instantly. These forms of ground offer the best opportunities.

The third dimension, *yuan*, is that of distance. Distance gauges the size of the area you must defend. A constricted (*ai*) position is one extreme. Strategically, a constricted opportunity is easily defended. Constricted positions concentrate your resources and focus your energy. You fill them by blocking every potential opening. Those who defend these positions cannot be attacked.

39Some field positions give you a barricade.
Get to these positions first.
You must occupy their southern, sunny heights in order to
await the enemy.
Sometimes the enemy occupies these areas first.
If so, entice him away.
Never go after him.

45Some field positions are too spread out.
Your force may seem equal to the enemy.
Still you will lose if you provoke a battle.
If you fight, you will not have any advantage.

49These are the six types of field positions.
Each battleground has its own rules.
As a commander, you must know where to go.
You must examine each position closely.

Some armies can be outmaneuvered. 2
Some armies are too lax.
Some armies fall down.
Some armies fall apart.
Some armies are disorganized.
Some armies must retreat.

7Know all six of these weaknesses.
They create weak timing and disastrous positions.
They all arise from the army's commander.

A barricaded (*xian*) position is the most obstructed extreme of the obstacle (*xian*) dimension. The opposite of an unobstructed position, a barricaded position, is good for defense but weak for movement and attack. Like a constricted position, it requires you to wait for your opponents to attack you. Unobstructed and barricaded positions offer opposite types of opportunities, but both can be used to your advantage if you understand the ground.

The spread-out (*yuan*) ground is the furthest extreme of the distance (*yuan*) dimension. It is the opposite of constricted ground. A spread-out position is unfocused, the weakest ground for both offense and defense. You never meet enemies in this position.

These six ground positions are extremes. Most positions combine these qualities to various degrees. When you recognize the nature of various positions, you immediately know your options and the best choices to make from any given position.

2 The six weaknesses in organization parallel the six types of ground. Each weakness is most dangerous on a specific type of ground. Being outmaneuvered is most dangerous in open positions, laxity in entangling positions, falling down in supporting positions, falling apart in constricted positions, disorganization in barricaded positions, and retreating in spread-out positions.

The *Bing-fa* attributes lack of organization solely to poor decision-making in a given ground position. You must recognize these weaknesses in yourself and in opponents.

¹⁰One general can command a force equal to the enemy.
Still his enemy outflanks him.
This means that his army can be outmaneuvered.

¹³Another can have strong soldiers but weak officers.
This means that his army is too lax.

¹⁵Another has strong officers but weak soldiers.
This means that his army will fall down.

¹⁷Another has subcommanders that are angry and defiant.
They attack the enemy and fight their own battles.
The commander cannot know the battlefield.
This means that his army will fall apart.

²¹Another general is weak and easygoing.
He fails to make his orders clear.
His officers and men lack direction.
This shows in his military formations.
This means that his army is disorganized.

²⁶Another general fails to predict the enemy.
He pits his small forces against larger ones.
His weak forces attack stronger ones.
He fails to pick his fights correctly.
This means that his army must retreat.

Problems with being outmaneuvered show up in unobstructed positions where free movement is possible. This is a problem with understanding the qualities of the ground.

Good methods require timely decision-making. In entangling positions you must wait until the time is right to attack.

Good decision-making requires skill in methods. Supportive positions arise from good decisions, but your skills maintain them.

Constricted terrain demands controlling the emotional climate. If you are emotional when you fight, you cannot maintain your focus. Those who lack focus attack opponents simply out of emotion. They lose track of what their goals are and crack under pressure.

When methods lack focus on the ground, fighters become sloppy and careless. They are unable to recognize their priorities. Problems for these types of people are most likely to arise in barricaded situations. For the barricade to hold, every point must be defended against penetration. Disorganized people always miss something.

When your decisions lack focus on change, you get caught by opponents in a spread-out position. Spread-out positions give you no leverage, allowing opponents to overpower you at the point of their choosing. You are caught in a spread-out position when you fail to predict an attack and spread out because you think you are safe.

³¹You must know all about these six weaknesses.
You must understand the philosophies that lead to defeat.
When a general arrives, you can know what he will do.
You must study each general carefully.

You must control your field position. 3
It will always strengthen your army.

³You must predict the enemy to overpower him and win.
You must analyze the obstacles, dangers, and distances.
This is the best way to command.

⁶Understand your field position before you go to battle.
Then you will win.
You can fail to understand your field position and meet
opponents.
Then you will fail.

¹⁰You must provoke battle when you will certainly win.
It doesn't matter what you are ordered.
The government may order you not to fight.
Despite that, you must always fight when you will win.

¹⁴Sometimes provoking a battle will lead to a loss.
The government may order you to fight.
Despite that, you must avoid battle when you will lose.

You must see these flaws in both yourself and others. People with these flaws are predictable, and nothing is more dangerous for a fighter than predictability. These six weaknesses are most likely to become a problem in dealing with certain types of field positions.

3 Success comes from making the right decisions about where to move. Every position you take is a stepping-stone to the next.

If you know your opponents and their weaknesses, you can predict the positions they will choose. The three dimensions of obstacles, dangers, and distance are the basis of your decisions.

Conforming to the ground is the key to advancing your position, and you can never meet an opponent successfully unless you understand the conditions of the ground. When you are challenged, your first responsibility as a martial artist is to know the precise nature of your position so you can know if you should defend or attack.

A mismatch of positions is like a mismatch of forces. When you are in a position of clear superiority, you must force a showdown. Even if personal or political considerations argue against a confrontation, once you recognize an opportunity you simply have no choice.

The reverse is also true. When you are in a position of clear inferiority, you must avoid meeting opponents on unfavorable ground. In making this decision, any desire for a confrontation is irrelevant.

[17]You must advance without desiring praise.
You must retreat without fearing shame.
The only correct move is to preserve your troops.
This is how you serve your country.
This is how you reward your nation.

Think of your soldiers as little children. 4
You can make them follow you into a deep river.
Treat them as your beloved children.
You can lead them all to their deaths.

[5]Some leaders are generous but cannot use their men.
They love their men but cannot command them.
Their men are unruly and disorganized.
These leaders create spoiled children.
Their soldiers are useless.

You may know what your soldiers will do in an attack. 5
You may not know if the enemy is vulnerable to attack.
You will then win only half the time.
You may know that the enemy is vulnerable to attack.
You may not know if your men have the capability of attack-
ing him.
You will still win only half the time.
You may know that the enemy is vulnerable to attack.
You may know that your men are ready to attack.
You may not, however, know how to position yourself in the
field for battle.
You will still win only half the time.

You cannot be aggressive simply to satisfy your ego. Nor can you allow fear to prevent you from being aggressive when your position is right for attack. The dynamics of competitive environments force you to move forward or backward in response to your relative positions. This is a matter of survival and a matter of success.

4 Those who teach the martial arts must care deeply about their students. Your decisions can put your followers into dangerous situations. Leaders must accept their responsibility and recognize that they have the power to affect the lives of others for better or worse.

Caring about people is more complicated than simply giving them what they want. If you truly care about people, you will do what enables their survival and success. Simply giving people what they immediately desire results in poor discipline, no focus on long-term goals, bad communication, and ultimate failure.

5 In the first chapter, the *Bing-fa* introduced comparison (*xiao*) as the only basis for knowing if a situation is "good" or "bad." Though the *Bing-fa* initially gave only five factors as the basis of comparison, since then you have learned about unity and focus, momentum and restraint, emptiness and fullness, adaptability, and so on. These concepts paint a more complete picture of the relative strengths and weaknesses of two opposing fighters. However, your condition is also defined by your situation on the ground relative to an opponent. The dimensions of field position are one aspect of this relative position. The topic of the next chapter, types of ground, completes that picture. It is equally important to understand your condition, the condition of your opponents, and your relative positions.

[11]You must know how to make war.
You can then act without confusion.
You can attempt anything.

[14]We say:
Know the enemy and know yourself.
Your victory will be painless.
Know the weather and the field.
Your victory will be complete.

✦ ✦ ✦

In strategy, the equation is simple. Knowledge is the basis of competition. Knowledge makes all movement and action possible. With the right knowledge, anything is possible.

Competitive knowledge can be categorized by its effects. Knowledge about your strength relative to that of the competition determines the difficulty in achieving success. Knowledge about trends, the topic of the next chapter, and the ground—which includes field position—determines the completeness of your success.

Chapter 11

九地

Types of Terrain: Recognize Nine Situations

The martial art school *Ba Gua Zhang* is based on the theory of
continuously changing in response to the situation at hand to
overcome an opponent with skill rather than brute force. This
philosophy could well describe all of martial arts, but the term *ba
gua* relates directly to the topic of this chapter. Dong Hai Chuan
founded the *Ba Gua Zhang* school in the Hebei Province of China in
the middle of the nineteenth century. However, the *ba gua* was first
connected to martial arts over 2,500 years ago in the *Bing-fa*.

Ba gua literally means "eight ways," originally referring to the
four major and four minor directions of a compass. It is used to
represent the relationships of eight "trigrams" of the *I Ching*, one
of the few Chinese texts older than the *Bing-fa*. Its eight directions
categorize the relationships of all natural phenomena. These eight
situations become nine because the center is part of the whole.

Sun Tzu uses the *ba gua* to graphically organize his strategy.
Four of the key factors in strategy—heaven, ground, the commander, and methods—are the primary directions, with the
fifth factor, philosophy, at the center. The four steps advancing a
position—knowledge (*zhi*), vision (*jian*), movement (*hang*), and
positioning (*xing*)—are the minor directions on the compass.

In this chapter, the *ba gua* is used to organize nine common
dynamic situations that arise in contests. The center is the home,
defensive position. The other eight situations are temporary conditions that arise with the passage of time and motion through space.

Types of Terrain

SUN TZU SAID:

Use the art of war. 1
Know when the terrain will scatter you.
Know when the terrain is easy.
Know when the terrain is disputed.
Know when the terrain is open.
Know when the terrain is intersecting.
Know when the terrain is dangerous.
Know when the terrain is bad.
Know when the terrain is confined.
Know when the terrain is deadly.

[11]Warring parties must sometimes fight inside their own territory.
This is scattering terrain.

[13]When you enter hostile territory, your penetration is shallow.
This is easy terrain.

[15]Some terrain gives you an advantageous position.
But it gives others an advantageous position as well.
This is disputed terrain.

Recognize Nine Situations

THE MARTIAL ARTIST HEARS:

1 Though the English terms used in translating the "nine grounds" are simple, the Chinese concepts are more complex. The first, *san*, means "scattered" or "diffuse." The next, *qing*, means "easy," "light," or "simple." The next, *zheng*, which you already know as "conflict," also means "to quarrel." The next, *jiao* (open), means literally "to cross," or "to join." The next, *qu*, means "to intersect" or "highway." The next, *chong* (dangerous), means literally "heavy" or "serious." The next, *pi* (bad), means literally "ruined" or "destroyed." The next, *wai* (confined), means "to encircle," or "to surround." The last, *si*, means "to die" or "extremity."

Scattering (*san*) conditions occur when you must defend your own territory against a large, skilled opponent. In terms of the *ba gua*, this is when you must defend the core of your position.

Easy (*qing*) conditions arise when you first move into an opponent's space using an opening. You initially meet little opposition.

There are situations in which both you and your opponent see the advantage in moving to the same spot. This creates conflict (*zheng*), which *Bing-fa* teaches is inherently costly in competition.

18You can use some terrain to advance easily.
Others can advance along with you.
This is open terrain.

21Everyone shares access to a given area.
The first one to arrive there can gather a larger group than
anyone else.
This is intersecting terrain.

24You can penetrate deeply into hostile territory.
Then many hostile cities are behind you.
This is dangerous terrain.

27There are mountain forests.
There are dangerous obstructions.
There are reservoirs.
Everyone confronts these obstacles on a campaign.
They make bad terrain.

32In some areas, the entry passage is narrow.
You are closed in as you try to get out of them.
In this type of area, a few people can effectively attack your
much larger force.
This is confined terrain.

36You can sometimes survive only if you fight quickly.
You will die if you delay.
This is deadly terrain.

Another translation for *jiao* is "crossing," which avoids the confusion with *tong* (open), the idea of unobstructed. The concept *jiao* means crossing an open area in a race with opponents.

Intersecting (*qu*) situations are those in which people can come together. These conditions make it possible to unite with others and form alliances. Not all other fighters are potential competitors; some are allies who can work with you for your mutual success.

Chong situations are dangerous because when you penetrate deeply into an opponent's space you expend your limited resources. You can then have your channels of support cut off.

Bad (*pi*) situations are dangerously obstructed (*xian*) because the path you thought to take is broken or impassable. In dynamic situations you need to move (*hang*) to make progress, but these conditions make movement difficult. Obstacles are the enemy of free movement because they slow you down.

Confined (*wai*) conditions are different from the constricted (*ai*) positions discussed in the last chapter. Confined situations are a temporary constraint. During a transition, your options are limited. Because your options are temporarily limited, you are increasingly vulnerable to opponents guessing what you are likely to do next.

Si (deadly or desperate) situations are the most dynamic of all. With each passing moment, you grow weaker while your opponent grows stronger. In these situations, if you hesitate you are lost.

39To be successful, you must control scattering terrain by
avoiding battle.
Control easy terrain by not stopping.
Control disputed terrain by not attacking.
Control open terrain by staying with the enemy's forces.
Control intersecting terrain by uniting with your allies.
Control dangerous terrain by plundering.
Control bad terrain by keeping on the move.
Control confined terrain by using surprise.
Control deadly terrain by fighting.

Go to an area that is known to be good for waging war. 2
Use it to cut off the enemy's contact between his front and
back lines.
Prevent his small parties from relying on his larger force.
Stop his strong divisions from rescuing his weak ones.
Prevent his officers from getting their men together.
Chase his soldiers apart to stop them from amassing.
Harass them to prevent their ranks from forming.

8When joining battle gives you an advantage, you must do it.
When it isn't to your benefit, you must avoid it.

10A daring soldier may ask:
"A large, organized enemy army and its general are coming.
What do I do to prepare for them?"

As you navigate each of these dynamic situations, your challenge is maintaining control. Your quick response is what prevents a fast-changing situation from degrading into chaos. For each of these situations, there is one and only one correct response that maintains your control. For example, in scattering situations, the necessary response is to avoid meeting the large opponent. In easy situations, the necessary response is to avoid stopping, and so on. By instantly responding correctly to the dynamic situation, you move the contest forward as another dynamic situation evolves. A contest is made of dynamic situations that arise one after another.

2 This lesson about dividing an opponent's forces addresses the "scattering" situation. When opponents are larger and stronger, you cannot simply block their blows. You must evade them and force them to defend themselves. Instead of losing your focus, you need to take the fight to your opponent. This is where the old adage "The best defense is a good offense" really works. Your aggression forces opponents back to defending their own position. This breaks their focus and their ability to organize their strength to attack you.

When do you strike at opponents and when do you avoid their blows? You avoid a larger opponent's blows until you can land your own.

Defense requires less effort than offense. Scattering situations only arise when you are facing a large, well-trained opponent. The basic prescription of "don't fight" is more difficult than it seems.

¹³Tell him:

"First seize an area that the enemy must have.
Then he will pay attention to you.
Mastering speed is the essence of war.
Take advantage of a large enemy's inability to keep up.
Use a philosophy of avoiding difficult situations.
Attack the area where he doesn't expect you."

You must use the philosophy of an invader. **3**
Invade deeply and then concentrate your forces.
This controls your men without oppressing them.

⁴Get your supplies from the riches of the territory.
They are sufficient to supply your whole army.

⁶Take care of your men and do not overtax them.
Your esprit de corps increases your momentum.
Keep your army moving and plan for surprises.
Make it difficult for the enemy to count your forces.
Position your men where there is no place to run.
They will then face death without fleeing.
They will find a way to survive.
Your officers and men will fight to their utmost.

¹⁴Military officers who are committed lose their fear.
When they have nowhere to run, they must stand firm.
Deep in enemy territory, they are captives.
Since they cannot escape, they will fight.

The only way to prevent stronger opponents from striking you is by using your speed to force them to defend. You want your opponents to "pay attention to you," which means that you want them dealing with your attacks rather than setting the agenda. Such a preemptive strike isn't a true attack in which you expect to hurt your opponent. These attacks force opponents to defend and react to your moves rather than controlling the situation themselves.

3 An attack scatters or distracts the defender, but it has the opposite effect on the invader (*ke*) or attacker. When you are committed to striking an opponent you focus your capabilities.

When you attack, you expend energy, but you can still gain relative strength if you weaken your opponent more.

Dangerous situations in which you invade an opponent's space have a powerful emotional effect that makes you stronger. Aggressiveness creates forward momentum, but you have to avoid getting too excited and careless. You must keep your opponent guessing about how strong you are. When you commit yourself—and your allies—to an aggressive course, your situation forces you to discover resources that you didn't even know you had. You and your allies have more energy and strength when you are attacking.

Once you commit yourself to attack, you stop worrying about what your opponents will do. When you commit yourself to striking your opponents, you find a way to make your attacks work. An aggressive philosophy commits you to using all your resources.

¹⁸Commit your men completely.
Without being posted, they will be on guard.
Without being asked, they will get what is needed.
Without being forced, they will be dedicated.
Without being given orders, they can be trusted.

²³Stop them from guessing by removing all their doubts.
Stop them from dying by giving them no place to run.

²⁵Your officers may not be rich.
Nevertheless, they still desire plunder.
They may die young.
Nevertheless, they still want to live forever.

²⁹You must order the time of attack.
Officers and men may sit and weep until their lapels are wet.
When they stand up, tears may stream down their cheeks.
Put them in a position where they cannot run.
They will show the greatest courage under fire.

Make good use of war. 4
This demands instant reflexes.
You must develop these instant reflexes.
Act like an ordinary mountain snake.
If people strike your head then stop them with your tail.
If they strike your tail then stop them with your head.
If they strike your middle then use both your head and tail.

The *Bing-fa* teaches you to trust your supporters. When people are completely committed to a cause and dependent on your mutual success, you don't have to worry about them. They are capable of managing themselves and doing whatever is necessary. No matter what your personal capabilities, trusting others makes you stronger.

You commit yourself to the group to remove their doubts about you. There is safety in numbers when the group is committed.

Every member of your group may not be individually powerful, but they all want to be successful and win recognition. Martial arts competition is dangerous for everyone, but everyone wants to be remembered for giving their best efforts.

When you challenge yourself and your followers, you can all rise to extraordinary heights. This doesn't mean that you won't have serious fears, especially as the moment of danger approaches. When you are afraid or uncertain, the secret to overcoming your fears is total commitment that leaves you no choice but to act.

4 In any contest, you constantly move from one dynamic situation to the next. As your situation changes, you must instantly recognize the new situation and change your response to react appropriately. The whole point of martial arts training is to learn how to instantly react to these situations as they occur. No matter how you are attacked, you can know instantly how to respond if your reflexes are correctly trained.

⁸A daring soldier asks:
"Can any army imitate these instant reflexes?"
We answer:
"It can."

¹²To command and get the most out of proud people, you
must study adversity.
People work together when they are in the same boat during
a storm.
In this situation, one rescues the other just as the right
hand helps the left.

¹⁵Use adversity correctly.
Tether your horses and bury your wagons' wheels.
Still, you can't depend on this alone.
An organized force is braver than lone individuals.
This is the art of organization.
Put the tough and weak together.
You must also use the terrain.

²²Make good use of war.
Unite your men as one.
Never let them give up.

The commander must be a military professional. 5
This requires confidence and detachment.
You must maintain dignity and order.
You must control what your men see and hear.
They must follow you without knowing your plans.

A good fighter looks for ways to bring the fight to his or her opponent. You might doubt that you can learn to instantly recognize and respond to all these different situations, but you can. This is just a matter of investing the time in the necessary training.

"Proud" is an interesting term because the Chinese term (*wu*) means "to boast." People are much less likely to worry about their egos when they are under pressure. The message is that you must put yourself and your supporters into challenging situations to get the most out of everyone's abilities. When you are working with others, you all work together better when you are focused on the goal.

Martial arts strategy teaches that sharing adversity as a group is a powerful tool. You can think you are totally committed to developing the martial arts, but group psychology magnifies that commitment. When others are watching and depending on you, you forget your personal doubts and fears. This the real power of being a member of a group. Being part of a group minimizes your weakness and amplifies your strengths in responding to a situation.

You must use good martial arts strategy. Within a group, unity and coordination are the sources of your success. One of the advantages of being in a group is that persistence assures your success.

5 To teach the martial arts, you must be dedicated to the martial arts. You must demonstrate self-assurance and objectivity. Your students must trust your seriousness and your priorities. You must pay attention to the impression you create. Others must respect your decisions without your having to explain your analysis.

⁶You can reinvent your men's roles.

You can change your plans.

You can use your men without their understanding.

⁹You must shift your campgrounds.

You must take detours from the ordinary routes.

You must use your men without giving them your strategy.

¹²A commander provides what is needed now.

This is like climbing high and being willing to kick away your ladder.

You must be able to lead your men deeply into different surrounding territory.

And yet, you can discover the opportunity to win.

¹⁶You must drive men like a flock of sheep.

You must drive them to march.

You must drive them to attack.

You must never let them know where you are headed.

You must unite them into a great army.

You must then drive them against all opposition.

This is the job of a true commander.

²³You must adapt to the different terrain.

You must adapt to find an advantage.

You must manage your people's affections.

You must study all these skills.

As the situation changes, you must respond by adjusting your student's assignments. You must be flexible in how you approach the situation. You shouldn't have to explain your decisions.

Students naturally fall into certain habits. When you are making decisions for students, you have to remain unpredictable in where you stay and where you go. You should keep your students guessing.

As a teacher, you focus everyone on making the next step successful. You ratchet up their commitment one step at a time, leaving them no way to easily back down. You prove your leadership by moving people out of their comfort zone and by opening them up to new possibilities. This is how a leader positions students to find their true potential.

The term *keui* that Sun Tzu uses for "drive" means simultaneously to "drive a carriage," "spur a horse," and "drive out." The idea is not slave driving, but guiding, prodding, and pushing students to move forward. Once you get students moving, it is easier to push them into becoming more aggressive. When people are moving together, their bonds grow and they become more dangerous to their opponents. This is your responsibility if you want to become a teacher.

The rules of adaptability require that you adjust your response to the current situation. Sun Tzu uses another term for "situation," *ching*, that has a second meaning of "feelings," or "affection," to reflect a parallel between managing people and situations.

Always use the philosophy of invasion. 6
Deep invasions concentrate your forces.
Shallow invasions scatter your forces.
When you leave your country and cross the border, you must take control.
This is always critical ground.
You can sometimes move in any direction.
This is always intersecting ground.
You can penetrate deeply into a territory.
This is always dangerous ground.
You penetrate only a little way.
This is always easy ground.
Your retreat is closed and the path ahead tight.
This is always confined ground.
There is sometimes no place to run.
This is always deadly ground.

[16]To use scattering terrain correctly, you must inspire your men's devotion.
On easy terrain, you must keep in close communication.
On disputed terrain, you try to hamper the enemy's progress.
On open terrain, you must carefully defend your chosen position.
On intersecting terrain, you must solidify your alliances.
On dangerous terrain, you must ensure your food supplies.
On bad terrain, you must keep advancing along the road.
On confined terrain, you must stop information leaks from your headquarters.
On deadly terrain, you must show what you can do by killing the enemy.

6 The shift between the nine dynamic situations is a process that has a beginning, a middle, and an end. At the beginning you must have a "philosophy of invasion," that is, you compete by forcing your opponents to defend their position instead of waiting for an attack and having your efforts dissipated in defense. *Ke*, or invasion, is a philosophy of aggression, putting opponents on the defensive. As you move forward, certain situations are likely to occur. At first, your advance is easy. Then you are faced with situations in which others can help you in intersecting situations. As you make more progress over time, the situation gets more challenging. This is a dangerous situation. For Sun Tzu it is axiomatic that if situations are easy, you haven't made much progress, but the more progress you make, the more difficult your situation becomes. Your success itself eventually limits your options, creating confined situations. In the end, however, it always comes down to a desperate situation, when you must prove what you can do.

In every situation, you must use human psychology as well as action. In scattering situations, focus unites the efforts of a group. In easy situations, communication keeps a group moving. In disputed situations, you can't attack your opponents, but you can harass them. In open situations, you must be cautious because your opponents can move against you. In intersecting situations, you have to support your supporters. In dangerous situations, you don't want to worry about your energy level. You need reserves of energy to keep going. In bad situations, you need to follow the easiest path available. In confined situations, you must keep your circumstances a secret, not giving your plan away. In desperate situations, you must fight to destroy your opponents.

²⁵Make your men feel like an army.
Surround them and they will defend themselves.
If they cannot avoid it, they will fight.
If they are under pressure, they will obey.

Do the right thing when you don't know your 7
different enemies' plans.
Don't attempt to meet them.

³You don't know the position of mountain forests, dangerous
obstructions, and reservoirs?
Then you cannot march the army.
You don't have local guides?
You won't get any of the benefits of the terrain.

⁷There are many factors in war.
You may lack knowledge of any one of them.
If so, it is wrong to take a nation into war.

¹⁰You must be able to control your government's war.
If you divide a big nation, it will be unable to put together a
large force.
Increase your enemy's fear of your ability.
Prevent his forces from getting together and organizing.

In the end, you win the dedication of your followers by putting them in situations in which they can shine. If you leave your supporters an excuse, you are inviting eventual failure. You must use dynamic situations to create total commitment.

7 The *Bing-fa* explains the nine situations in terms of knowledge, vision, movement, and positioning. To be successful, you must use vision to see an opening in your opponent's plans.

Vision comes from knowledge of the physical ground. You cannot see an opportunity worthy of a battle unless you have an understanding of the area in which you are operating. Without knowledge and the resulting vision, you cannot move or use positioning to get the benefit of the situation on the ground.

Though all four skills—knowledge, vision, movement, and positioning—are necessary, knowledge is the key to everything. Without knowing what you are doing, you cannot be successful.

The four skills determine your progress in a given situation, but the group depends on unity. If you can divide your opponent's forces while keeping your group united and focused, your ability to take advantage of a situation becomes more certain. Division works both physically and as an emotional and psychological tool.

¹⁴Do the right thing and do not arrange outside alliances
before their time.
You will not have to assert your authority prematurely.
Trust only yourself and your self-interest.
This increases the enemy's fear of you.
You can make one of his allies withdraw.
His whole nation can fall.

²⁰Distribute rewards without worrying about having a system.
Halt without the government's command.
Attack with the whole strength of your army.
Use your army as if it were a single man.

²⁴Attack with skill.
Do not discuss it.
Attack when you have an advantage.
Do not talk about the dangers.
When you can launch your army into deadly ground, even if
it stumbles, it can still survive.
You can be weakened in a deadly battle and yet be stronger
afterward.

³⁰Even a large force can fall into misfortune.
If you fall behind, however, you can still turn defeat into victory.
You must use the skills of war.
To survive, you must adapt yourself to your enemy's purpose.
You must stay with him no matter where he goes.
It may take a thousand miles to kill the general.
If you correctly understand him, you can find the skill to do it.

In the realm of unity, Sun Tzu is deeply suspicious of alliances of convenience—that is, those that are not based on a shared philosophy. Alliances between separate groups are inherently difficult because these groups have different goals. Add to this the idea that large groups are inherently slower than small ones, and alliances become even more difficult to manage. Sun Tzu teaches that the best strategy is to attack alliances rather than depend on them.

One of the most important advantages of working outside alliances is that you don't have to deal with the politics of larger organizations. A small group can share the rewards, eliminate unnecessary waste, focus its resources, and enjoy the general benefits of unity.

Your ability to attack—that is, to force your opponents to defend— depends on your training. Since training depends on knowledge (*zhi*), you keep your opponents ignorant of your plans. You also keep your people unaware of the dangers to keep them focused on the task at hand. You use the dangers of desperate (*si*) situations to purposefully focus your abilities on the task at hand. Though desperate situations are inherently difficult, you can meet the problems that they present and become more powerful for that experience.

The larger reality is that even when you are powerful and united, your group can fail. However, a central precept of the *Bing-fa* is that you must limit your potential failures so that you can recover from them. Normally, you do this by keeping your movements small and close. This limits your potential losses, but even a large mistake is not a death sentence. Even big moves can be successful if they are based on a superior understanding of your situation.

Manage your government correctly at the start of a war. 8
Close your borders and tear up passports.
Block the passage of envoys.
Encourage the halls of power to rise to the occasion.
You must use any means to put an end to politics.
Your enemy's people will leave you an opening.
You must instantly invade through it.

[8]Immediately seize a place that they love.
Do it quickly.
Trample any border to pursue the enemy.
Use your judgment about when to fight.

[12]Doing the right thing at the start of war is like
approaching a woman.
Your enemy's men must open the door.
After that, you should act like a streaking rabbit.
The enemy will be unable to catch you.

8 Skilled fighters learn to manage those in authority over them. You must control your physical boundaries and deny people access. You control the flow of information that your opponent gets. You distance yourself from those concerned only with their own interests. You must champion the shared goals of the group. Wait for a clear opening to move decisively. When the opportunity arises, waste no time in taking advantage of it.

You must threaten your opponents' weak points, where they are concerned about protecting themselves. Your speed is the key. Don't let imaginary barriers prevent you from challenging opponents. Your training is the key to picking the right timing.

Even though the *Bing-fa* provides a detailed rule book for martial arts strategy, it teaches that your methods (*fa*) are art as well as science. Using strategy demands the subtlety and sensitivity of a man wooing a woman. This is especially true in understanding the subtleties of the nine dynamic situations that you must master.

Chapter 12

Attacking With Fire: Leverage the Environment

In traditional Chinese martial arts, there are five types of weapons: throwing/shooting weapons such as knives, long weapons such as spears, short weapons such as swords, soft weapons such as whips, and double weapons such as claws. None of these weapons are strategic. Fire *is* strategic because it targets your opponent's position. It is an analogy for all attacks on a strategic position, which are the basis for all your battles, not just a single confrontation.

As an environmental weapon, fire depends on the ground and climate supports it. More importantly, you don't control environmental weapons directly. Their direction, speed, and duration depend on the environment itself. Though this chapter deals with the dangers of the environment, it teaches the discipline you must maintain in the face of any type of attack.

Vigilance starts by recognizing where you might become a target. Strategic attacks not only threaten you personally; they can threaten your resources, supporters, assets, and so on. The best method of countering these threats is to remove yourself from dangerous conditions long before they can hurt you. When you are threatened by the environment, your safety depends upon reacting correctly. The impersonal forces of the environment are dangerous on their own, but the danger is magnified if you panic. Panic leaves you open to more direct attacks by other opponents.

In this sense, fire is also a metaphor for the fire of rage, the most dangerous environmental weapon of all.

Attacking With Fire

SUN TZU SAID:

There are five ways of attacking with fire. 1
The first is burning troops.
The second is burning supplies.
The third is burning supply transport.
The fourth is burning storehouses.
The fifth is burning camps.

7To make fire, you must have the resources.
To build a fire, you must prepare the raw materials.

9To attack with fire, you must be in the right season.
To start a fire, you must have the time.

11Choose the right season.
The weather must be dry.

13Choose the right time.
Pick a season when the grass is as high as the side of a cart.

15You can tell the proper days by the stars in the night sky.
You want days when the wind rises in the morning.

Leverage the Environment

1 In giving you the targets for fire, the *Bing-fa* makes it clear that strategic attacks are not just aimed at people. First are people (*ren*). Next, in keeping with the *Bing-fa*'s economic focus, are supplies (*ji*), literally stores or savings. Next is the transportation of supplies (*zi*). Next is storehouses (*ku*). Finally, you have camps, literally groupings (*dui*). Each of these is a focal point for an attack.

Your opponents cannot create the opportunity to target your strategic position. Rivals can only use resources found in the environment.

The changes in climate determine when you are vulnerable to these attacks. Opponents can work to use your environment against you.

You need to know when conditions are dangerous to you or your opponents. The sources of danger might exist all around you.

You cannot create the right conditions for environmental attacks; you must wait until the right conditions present themselves.

You can, however, observe the conditions developing to support these types of attacks and choose a time when forces support them.

Everyone attacks with fire. 2
People can create five different situations with fire and you
must be able to adjust to them.

3People can start a fire inside the enemy's camp.
Then they attack the enemy's periphery.

5People launch a fire attack, but the enemy remains calm.
They will then wait and not attack.

7The fire reaches its height.
Opponents will follow its path if they can.
If they can't follow it, they stay where they are.

10Spreading fires on the outside of camp can kill.
People can't always get fire inside the enemy's camp.
They take their time in spreading it.

13People set fire when the wind is at their back.
They won't attack into the wind.
Daytime winds last a long time.
Night winds fade quickly.

17Every army must know how to adjust to the five possible
attacks by fire.
Use many men to guard against them.

2 Martial arts strategy teaches that a threat can come from any direction. You must recognize the five different forms that environmental threats take and know how to counter them.

The core leader or belief holding a group together can be attacked. Then enemies will attempt to pick off the members of a group.

If you remain calm during crises, you are safe. The real danger to your strategic position occurs when you panic.

Every strategic crisis will reach a peak. During these periods, you must avoid leaving your opponents an opening. Without an opening, your opponents cannot bring you down.

People can sow the seeds of small problems all around you. This is common when opponents cannot hurt you directly. You must defend yourself patiently from this type of attack.

You are in danger when the trends go against you. This is a matter of timing. When your luck changes, you are safe. When your bad luck is well known, it can last a long time. When no one knows about it, your luck can change quickly.

You can defend against any form of attack on your position if you know what to expect. You must continually analyze your surroundings and use vigilance to protect yourself.

People who use fire to assist their attacks are clever. 3
Water can add force to an attack.
People can also use water to disrupt an enemy.
It does not, however, take his resources.

You win in battle by getting the opportunity to attack. 4
It is dangerous if you fail to study how to accomplish this
achievement.
As commander, you cannot waste your opportunities.

4We say:
A wise leader plans success.
A good general studies it.
If there is little to be gained, don't act.
If there is little to win, do not use your men.
If there is no danger, don't fight.

10As the leader, you cannot let your anger interfere with the
success of your forces.
As commander, you cannot let yourself become enraged
before you go to battle.
Join the battle only when it is in your advantage to act.
If there is no advantage in joining a battle, stay put.

14Anger can change back into happiness.
Rage can change back into joy.
A nation once destroyed cannot be brought back to life.
Dead men do not return to the living.

3 The *Bing-fa* teaches you to be wary of opponents who use the environment. Changes in the environment can add ferocity to any attack. Your progress is easy to stop if the climate is against you. Forces in the environment can seriously damage you.

4 Many people are uncomfortable using environmental attacks against their opponents. However, like all competitive tools that you have, you must make the most of these attacks when an opportunity presents itself. You cannot afford to disregard them.

These attacks (and all competitive attacks) require the proper foresight and deliberation in thinking about your position. They should not be used lightly. Remember that attacking is always costly; even fire or environmental attacks have costs. You must make sure that you have something real to gain before trying to damage a rival's position. Victory is making winning pay in terms of your position!

The real masters of martial arts strategy are always in control of their emotions so that they can make good decisions. Your decision to meet a challenge must be made with a clear head and a quiet heart because your reputation is important. You gain nothing by lashing out at opponents in anger. If you have nothing to gain, you should never attack the position of a potential rival.

The *Bing-fa* teaches that emotions change like the weather. Today's rival can become tomorrow's ally. When actions are destructive, you cannot take them back. What you lose, you can lose forever. Martial artists control their emotions and use their heads.

[18]This fact must make a wise leader cautious.
A good general is on guard.

[20]Your philosophy must be to keep the nation peaceful and
the army intact.

✦ ✦ ✦

You cannot be too sensitive to hurt an opponent's position, and you must always defend your own position against these attacks.

Using these attacks and defending against them is necessary if you want to improve your strategic position over the long run.

Chapter 13

Using Spies: Know Your Opponents

The final topic of Sun Tzu's *Bing-fa* is the importance of knowledge. This lesson applies to issues beyond martial arts strategy. Everything you have learned thus far builds to the idea that good-quality information is the most important element of creating success in life and the martial arts. Information is the source of all strategy, but you can only get the most valuable information from having the right contacts. Strategy replaces force and effort with information. Information comes from knowing other people.

Martial arts competition is difficult and dangerous. Without the right information, you cannot properly prepare to meet your opponents. Most people spend too little time and effort learning about their opposition. The best fighters are different because they place a premium on knowing others. You must build and maintain a network of contacts if you want to be as successful as you can be.

Information can be misleading, especially when it comes from only one kind of source. Good strategy requires that martial artists build a wide variety of contacts to provide a well-rounded view of their potential opposition. Sun Tzu teaches specifically that five different types of sources are needed to create a complete view.

Developing and maintaining a good network of sources requires a special set of strategic skills. Without the right social skills, you will never get the information you need. Without the information you need, you cannot develop a successful strategy. In many ways, Sun Tzu saves his most important lessons for the end of his book.

Using Spies

SUN TZU SAID:

All successful armies require thousands of men. 1
They invade and march thousands of miles.
Whole families are destroyed.
Other families must be heavily taxed.
Every day, a large amount of money must be spent.

^{6}Internal and external events force people to move.
They are unable to work while on the road.
They are unable to find and hold a useful job.
This affects 70 percent of thousands of families.

^{10}You can watch and guard for years.
Then a single battle can determine victory in a day.
Despite this, bureaucrats worship the value of their salary
money too dearly.
They remain ignorant of the enemy's condition.
The result is cruel.

^{15}They are not leaders of men.
They are not servants of the state.
They are not masters of victory.

Know Your Opponents

THE MARTIAL ARTIST HEARS:

1 The strategy of martial arts uses information to control the potential costs of competition. Mastering the martial arts requires a tremendous investment in time and effort. The risks of battle are a lesson in life. No matter how much effort you invest, you cannot assure your success. Success is always costly.

Life offers many distractions from using good martial arts strategy. Everyone has to make a living. You don't want martial arts to become a distraction from the other parts of your life. You want your mastery of martial arts to make your life richer, not poorer.

Mastering the martial arts teaches you to be careful and patient in awaiting opportunities. The right opportunity can change your life. Money is worthless if you remain ignorant of your opportunities. Nothing is more important in life or in battle than having the right information at the right time. Because of this, martial arts strategy teaches that true knowledge is more important than money.

Without the right knowledge, you will always be a student and never a master. Without focusing on knowledge, you will never control your life. Without a focus on knowledge, you will never find success.

[18]You need a creative leader and a worthy commander.
You must move your troops to the right places to beat others.
You must accomplish your attack and escape unharmed.
This requires foreknowledge.
You can obtain foreknowledge.
You can't get it from demons or spirits.
You can't see it from professional experience.
You can't check it with analysis.
You can only get it from other people.
You must always know the enemy's situation.

You must use five types of spies. 2
You need local spies.
You need inside spies.
You need double agents.
You need doomed spies.
You need surviving spies.

[7]You need all five types of spies.
No one must discover your methods.
You will then be able to put together a true picture.
This is the commander's most valuable resource.

[11]You need local spies.
Get them by hiring people from the countryside.

[13]You need inside spies.
Win them by subverting government officials.

There are two critical and central ideas here. First, only timely information makes your decisions effective. The strategic processes of *Bing-fa* create success only if they are based on timely information. Second, all timely information comes from human contact, that is, from knowing what others are planning. The chaos of competition is not predictable. Mastering martial arts or making progress in life is a matter of preparing for the future. Your preparation cannot be built on fantasy, but upon the real world and the real people in it. People's decisions create the future. In competition, you must know your opponents and their situation to be successful.

2 Though translated as "spies," the Chinese character Sun Tzu uses, *gaan*, means "a space between," that is, a go-between, a conduit of information. You need these go-betweens to learn about the environment in which you meet opponents, how your opponents think, the methods that opponents use, how to transmit misleading information, and how to get timely information.

A single viewpoint about an opponent is misleading. People will tell you what they want you to hear or what you want to hear. You must overcome your preconceptions about others to learn about them. You must protect your information channels and contacts.

Some people know your battleground better than you do. You must make contact with people with experience in different areas.

Insiders are close to your opponents and those who work with them. Only these insiders know how your opponents think.

¹⁵You need double agents.
Discover enemy agents and convert them.

¹⁷You need doomed spies.
Deceive professionals into being captured.
Let them know your orders.
They will then take those orders to your enemy.

²¹You need surviving spies.
Someone must return with a report.

Your job is to build a complete army. 3
No relations are as intimate as the ones with spies.
No rewards are too generous for spies.
No work is as secret as that of spies.

⁵If you aren't clever and wise, you can't use spies.
If you aren't fair and just, you can't use spies.
If you can't see the small subtleties, you won't get the truth
from spies.

⁸Pay attention to small, trifling details!
Spies are helpful in every area.

¹⁰Spies are the first to hear information, so they must not
spread information.
Spies who give your location or talk to others must be killed
along with those to whom they have talked.

Double agents come from converting opponents' sources of information. You want to learn from those who trained them.

Unlike the others, doomed spies send information rather than receive it. You use them to communicate a desired impression to opponents. You use relationships—and damage them—to control opponents' perceptions and therefore shape their plans.

Surviving spies are those who have met an opponent recently and can give you the latest information on his or her situation.

3 To be completely successful in combat and in life, you must seek out information on potential opponents. You must make your information sources into your best friends. You must be willing to invest in these relationships to get good, reliable information. You need to know what no one else knows.

The information you get from people is always flawed and incomplete. You must put together what makes sense and what doesn't for yourself, without prejudice and prior assumptions.

You must pay attention to the details and gather small bits of information about your opponents to put together a complete picture.

You must have information sources that you can trust to keep your confidence. You don't want your opponents to know what you know about them. If your contacts give out confidential information about you, you are better off without them.

You may want to attack an army's position. 4
You may want to attack a certain fortification.
You may want to kill people in a certain place.
You must first know the guarding general.
You must know his left and right flanks.
You must know his hierarchy.
You must know the way in.
You must know where different people are stationed.
You must demand this information from your spies.

10You want to know the enemy spies in order to convert
them into your men.
You must find sources of information and bribe them.
You must bring them in with you.
You must obtain them as double agents and use them as
your emissaries.

14Do this correctly and carefully.
You can contact both local and inside spies and obtain their
support.
Do this correctly and carefully.
You create doomed spies by deceiving professionals.
You can use them to give false information.
Do this correctly and carefully.
You must have surviving spies capable of bringing you infor-
mation at the right time.

4 When you plan to meet specific opponents, you need specific information about their current situation and condition. You want to understand how they defend themselves and the attacks to which they are most susceptible. You want to know who your opponents' teachers are. You want to know with whom they are working. You must understand their personal priorities. You must know how they position themselves. When you know about their specific talents, you can overcome them. When you know their specific form, you can outmaneuver them. Your knowledge is the key.

The best place to start developing contacts is with people who are in contact with your opponents. You must find a way to befriend these people. You must make it clear that you appreciate their help and support. They must find it rewarding to help you. You can use these people to get information from your opponents and to misinform them about your intentions and capabilities.

The *Bing-fa* teaches that building an information network must be done with extreme care. You want to get to know people without it being apparent who your contacts are. The more secretive you can be about your sources of information, the less likely it is that your opponents will be able to tap into them. You sometimes need to sacrifice a relationship to provide misinformation to an opponent. If you are quiet and methodical in building up and maintaining your relationships, you can have contacts everywhere within your community who can report the latest developments.

²¹These are the five different types of intelligence work.
You must be certain to master them all.
You must be certain to create double agents.
You cannot afford to be too cost conscious in creating these
double agents.

This technique created the success of ancient Shang. 5
This is how the Shang held their dynasty.

³You must always be careful of your success.
Learn from Lu Ya of Shang.

⁵Be a smart commander and a good general.
You do this by using your best and brightest people for spying.
This is how you achieve the greatest success.
This is how you meet the necessities of war.
The whole army's position and ability to move depends on
these spies.

You must suspect information that comes from only one source. Act only on information that you can verify. You must especially know your opponents' points of view. Most people spend too little time and effort learning what their rivals think. Good information can eliminate many of the risks and challenges of competition.

5 In the martial arts and every other field, successful people are serious students of history who study the success of others.

Masters of the martial arts start as students who seek to emulate the individuals who serve as their role models.

In martial arts strategy, making the best possible decisions is your central responsibility. Making winning decisions is much more a matter of information than of strength. You can only meet the challenges you face if you are armed with knowledge. Your skill in the martial arts and your progress through life depend on whom you choose to trust as your source of knowledge.

Glossary of the *Bing-fa's* Key Concepts

The purpose of this glossary is to define the central ideas in Sun Tzu's strategic system. It offers a standard vocabulary for key terms, describing how Sun Tzu uses specific Chinese characters to express his concepts and their relationships. We give his Chinese characters Chinese names to emphasize that they differ from the English terms used in translation. These Chinese names come from standard Pinyin (Mandarin) but without the tone numbers. Alternate Pinyin or Cantonese terms are sometimes used so that each concept has a unique name. Though based on Chinese, these terms are not meant to represent any actual Chinese spoken dialect.

AI: 狹 *narrow, constricted*: a confined space or narrow niche; one of six field positions; the limited extreme of the dimension YUAN, distance; opposite of GUANG, wide.

BAO: 賞 *treasure, reward*: the necessary compensation for success; winning is not beating the competition, but producing a reward; victory must pay.

BEI: 北 *flee, northward*: run away without fighting; one of six weaknesses of an organization; opposite of JEUN, advance.

BENG: 崩 *split apart, collapse*: fall apart over time; one of six weaknesses of an organization.

BI: 避 *evade, avoid*: the strategy used by small competitors when facing large opponents.

BIAN: 變 *change, transform*: transition from one condition to another; the ability to adapt to different situations.

BING: 兵 *weapons, soldiers, war*: competition; the use of force.

BU: 不 *no, not*: negates the meaning of the following ideogram; the character that provides the opposing idea for concepts that have no natural opposite.

BU ZHI: 不知 *not to know, ignorance*: a failure to understand or to gather information; the cardinal sin in BING-FA; opposite of ZHI, knowledge.

CHENG: 城 *city*: fortified town; a strong position that is costly to attack.

CHI: 治 *govern, rule, control*: literally, to harness a river; to manage or govern people or situations; the opposite of JUAN, disorder.

CHING: 情 *feelings, affection, love, situation*: the bonds of relationship that must be managed like other situations.

CHONG: 重 *serious, heavy*: requiring effort and skill; the situation of being deeply committed to a campaign, with opposition behind; one of nine situations or types of terrain.

CONG: 從 *follow*: to obey, to submit to, and to trail; opposite of GWO, pass.

CU: 趨 *hurry*: to rush into or to be attracted to; a dangerous method to move; opposite of DAI, wait.

DA: 大 *big, large*: forces that are much larger than opponents' forces; opposite of SIU, small.

DAI: 待 *wait, await*: staying in place patiently; inaction when there is no opportunity; the opposite of CU, hurry.

DI: 地 *ground, earth, situation, condition*: a specific place, condition, or situation; where one competes and simultaneously the prize of competition; one of five key factors in competitive analysis; the opposite of TIAN, heaven.

DIE: 至 *arrive, reach, stop*: end of movement to a destination or goal; opposite of HEUI, to go.

DIK: 敵 *enemy, opponent*: someone who desires the same position; a competitor.

DUI: 隊 *group, team, troop*: a grouping of people; one of the five targets of fire attacks.

DUN: 鈍 *blunt, dull*: a slow mental attitude; opposite of RIU, sharp.

FA: 法 *method, laws*: procedures, techniques, steps to accomplish a goal; one of the five key factors in analysis; the realm of groups who must follow procedures; the conceptual opposite of JIANG, the general, who is free from law because he makes the law.

FAN: 反 *reverse, flip, double back, double agent*: to turn around in direction; to change a situation; to switch a person's allegiance; one of five types of spies.

FEI: 費 *waste, waste time, consume*: to expend limited resources; the result of unnecessary conflict.

FEN: 分 *divide, separate*: to break apart a larger force; opposite of HAP, to join, and ZHUAN, to concentrate.

FENG: 風 *wind, custom, fashion*: the pressure of environmental forces; a necessary ingredient for fire or environmental attacks.

GAAN: 間 *spy, conduit*: literally, opening between; go-between; channel of information.

GAI: 計 *plan, planning*: analysis of a situation; used as a combination of ZHI (knowledge) and JIAN (vision); used in combination with GUI (deception) to create GUI GAI, deceptive plans, tricks, or traps.

GONG: 攻 *attack, strike*: any action against an opponent; a movement into new territory; the opposite of SHOU, to defend.

GONG CHENG: 攻城 *siege, strike city*: any action against an entrenched position; one of the five basic attacks; the least desirable form of attack.

GUA: 懸 *hanging, suspended, entangling*: a position that cannot be returned to; any condition that leaves no place to go; one of six field positions.

GUANG: 廣 *wide*: lacking constraint; ground form opposite of AI, narrow.

GUI: 詭 *deception, bluffing, illusion*: misleading the competition; an attack on an opponent's JAING, vision; the essence of war.

GUO: 國 *nation*: state; the productive part of an organization; the seat of political power; the entity that controls an army or competitive part of the organization.

GWAI: 貴 *expensive*: costly in terms of money or resources. Closely related conceptually to the idea of FEI, to consume or waste.

Gwo: 過 *pass, pass through, go across*: to exceed or surpass; opposite of CONG, follow.

HAAM: 陷 *sink, plunge, trap*: fall down or into; one of six weaknesses of organizations.

HANG: 行 *act, march, go, walk*: action toward a position or goal. Used as a near synonym for DONG, act.

HAP: 合 *join*: to unite with allies to create a larger force; opposite of FEN, divide.

HEI: 氣 *spirit, air, steam, gas*: something insubstantial; a characteristic of DONG, movement, so opponents cannot know a position.

HEUI: 去 *go away*: to depart; to leave an area; opposite of DIE, arrive.

HUO: 火 *fire*: the only weapon whose use Sun Tzu details; used as an analogy for attacks in general and environmental attacks in particular.

JANG: 正 *straight, right, proper, correct*: the expected normal behavior; the standard approach; the opposite of QI, unusual.

JEUN: 進 *advance, make progress*: to move forward in a campaign; opposite of BEI, retreat.

JI: 糧 *savings, stores, accumulate*: resources that have been stored up; one of the five targets of fire attacks.

JIAN: 見 *vision, to see, foreseeing*: the skill of the general in observing TIAN, heaven and finding an advantage, LI.

JIANG: 將 *general, commander*: the leader of an army; the decision-maker in a competitive unit; the superior of officers and men; one of the five key factors in analysis. The conceptual opposite of FA, the laws, which do not require decisions.

JIAO: 來 *meeting, joining, crossing*: to come together; to intersect; an open situation that encourages a race; one of nine situations or types of terrain.

JIE: 節 *restraint; to restrain*: to withhold action until the proper time; a companion concept to SHI, momentum.

JIK: 直 *direct, straight*: a straight or obvious path to a goal; opposite of YU, detour.

JING: 政 *government, political affairs*: the force of authority; the ability to organize.

JIU: 九 *nine, many*: used to indicate many different types as well as the specific number.

JIU: 久 *long time, delay*: avoiding action for a period of time; lacking immediacy.

JUAN: 亂 *chaos, disorder*: conditions that cannot be predicted exactly; the natural state of confusion arising from competition; one of six weaknesses of an organization; opposite of CHI, control.

JUN: 軍 *army, armed*: pertaining to a military force; the most dangerous type of ZHENG, conflict.

KE: 客 *guest, invader*: inside an opponent's territory; one who consumes resources.

KEUI: 驅 *drive, expel*: to motivate people to move and to keep them moving.

KU: 庫 *houses, storehouses*: places where supplies can be stockpiled; one of the five targets for fire attacks.

LEI: 力 *force*: power in the simplest sense; with dominant energy.

LI: 利 *advantage, benefit*: an opportunity arising from having a better position relative to opponents; a key characteristic of position.

LIANG: 糧 *provisions, resources, food*: necessary supplies, most commonly food; one of the five targets of fire attacks.

LING: 令 *command*: orders or the act of ordering subordinates.

LIU: 陸 *plateau, land, continent*: one of the five types of land; analogy for level, solid, and certain ground.

LU: 奪 *seize*: to catch; to capture; to imprison; taking control of desired ground to discourage an opponent's attack.

LUE: 掠 *plunder, rob, take by force*: gathering provisions from enemy territory.

NEI: 内 *inside, internal*: within a territory or organization; an insider; one of five types of spies; opposite of WAI, external.

PI: 圮 *ruined, bad*: destroyed; terrain that is broken and difficult to traverse; one of the nine situations or types of terrain.

PO: 破 *broken, divide*: an attack on QUAN, whole, and the opposite of YI, oneness.

QI: 奇 *strange, unusual, odd, improper, surprise*: the unexpected; the surprising; result of the creative impulse; the opposite of JANG, straight.

QI JANG: 奇正 *innovation*: a combination of QI, the unusual, and JANG, the standard; the change that creates SHI, momentum.

QING: 輕 *easy, light*: requiring little effort; a situation that requires little effort; one of nine situations or types of terrain; opposite of CHONG, dangerous or serious.

QU: 衢 *highway, intersecting*: a situation or type of ground that facilitates travel; one of nine types of terrain.

QUAN: 全 *complete, whole*: the sense of lacking nothing needed or being finished; creates YI, oneness or unity; arises from TAO, philosophy; the opposite of PO, divided.

REN: 人 *man, men, person, people*: members of an army or organization; individuals; one of the five targets of fire attacks.

RIU: 鋭 *sharp, keen*: acuity of mind; the fine point of a weapon; opposite of DUN, dull.

SAN: 散 *scatter, scattering*: to disperse; a situation that causes a force to scatter; one of nine conditions or types of terrain.

SAT: 壹 *full, substantial, wealthy, strong*: the state of being crowded; the opposite of XU, empty.

SHAANG: 生 *birth, born*: creation; one of five types of spies; opposite of SI, dead.

SHAN: 善 *good, virtuous*: acting correctly; making the correct decisions.

SHAN: 山 *mountain, hill, peak*: one of four types of land; analogy for uneven places with peaks and valleys.

SHANG: 上 *above, up, before, better than*: superiority in time or position; opposite of XIA, below.

SHAO: 寡 *few*: a small force or group; a weak point exhibiting the characteristic of XU, emptiness; opposite of ZHONG, crowd.

SHEN: 神 *spirit, ghost, supernatural being*: the essence of a person or group of people.

SHI: 勢 *influence, force, momentum*: used specifically by Sun Tzu as the result of QI JANG, innovation; in some ways the opposite of JIE, restraint.

SHII: 弛 *relax, loosen*: too lax; too easygoing; one of six weaknesses of an army.

SHOU: 守 *defend, defense*: to guard or keep a possession; to remain in a position; the opposite of GONG, attack.

SHU: 數 *count, calculate, number*: mathematical evaluation of a situation.

SHUI: 水 *water, fluid*: one of four types of land; analogy for fluid conditions that change rapidly.

SI: 死 *death, dead, deadly, extreme*: termination of life or efforts; an extreme situation in which the only option is to fight; one of nine situations or types of terrain; one of five types of spies; opposite of SAANG, birth.

SING: 勝 *victory, to win*: success in an endeavor; winning a battle; the only goal of BING-FA; it produces more than it consumes.

SIU: 少 *little, small*: forces that are small in relative size; the opposite of DA, big.

SOU: 走 *misstep, go astray*: used to describe being outmaneuvered; one of six weaknesses of an army.

SUO: 所 *place, location*: a specific position on the ground, common term to indicate a position.

TAO: 道 *philosophy, way*: a system of thought; literally "road" or "path," as in the "path to victory"; one of five key factors in analysis.

TIAN: 天 *heaven*: divine providence; climate; weather; trends that change over time; one of five key factors in analysis.

TING: 聽 *listen, understand, obey*: to gather knowledge (ZHI).

TONG: 通 *open, unobstructed, expert*: without obstacles or barriers; available for easy movement; accepting of new ideas; one of six field positions; opposite of XIAN, obstructed.

WAI: 外 *external, outside*: not within a territory or organization; an outsider; a remote perspective that gives an objective view; opposite of NEI, internal.

WAN: 萬 *myriad*: a large, complex group; a big organization.

WEI: 圍 *surround, confined*: to encircle; the normal tactic for a much larger force encapsulating a smaller one; the characteristic of a special transitional situation in which a larger force can be attacked by a smaller one; one of nine situations or types of terrain.

WU: 吳 *boast, an ancient Chinese kingdom*: name of the kingdom for which Sun Tzu was hired as a general.

XIA: 下 *below, under, following*: a lower position or status; opposite of SHANG, above.

XIAN: 險 *obstacles, obstructed*: containing obstacles; one of six field positions; opposite of TONG, unobstructed.

XIANG: 鄉 *countryside, local*: having local knowledge; knowing a specific ground; one of five types of spies.

XIAO: 效 *learn, compare, proofread*: to compare qualities between two competing opponents; to double-check.

XIN: 心 *feeling, emotion*: a visceral reaction to JIAN, vision necessary to inspire HANG, movement; an important component of esprit de corps; never a sufficient cause for GONG, attack.

XING: 形 *form, position*: a shape or condition of DI, the ground; using the benefits of the ground; formations of troops; bringing together resources at a specific time and place; one of the four key skills in making progress.

XU: 處 *emptiness, insubstantial, weakness*: devoid of force; identifying a point of attack or a path of movement; full of need; needy, poor; the opposite of SAT, full.

YANG: 陽 *south, sunny hillside, male principle*: used to mean a strong position; opposite of YIN, north, shady hillside.

YAO: 事 *profession, business, affair, to serve*: a thing that needs to be done; skill; ability; responsibility.

YI: 一 *one, oneness*: the first number, used by Sun Tzu to indicate unity; opposite of ZHONG, crowd, in one sense, and PO, divided, in another.

YIN: 陰 *north, shady hillside, the female principle*: used to mean a weak position; opposite of YANG, south, sunny hillside.

YONG: 勇 *brave, bravery*: courage of conviction; willingness to act on vision; one of the six characteristics of a leader.

YOU: 誘 *entice*: to lure an opponent away from a position; a method of GUI, deception.

YU: 迂 *detour*: the indirect or unsuspected path to a goal; the more difficult path to opportunity; opposite of JIK, direct.

YUAN: 遠 *distance, far, spread-out*: remote from current location; occupying positions that are not close to one another; one of six field positions; one of the three dimensions for evaluating opportunities; the most extreme case of this dimension.

YUE: 曰 *say, called*: to talk, to discuss; used to identify key concepts that require discussion in the original Chinese.

YUN: 均 *equal, fair*: evenly balanced situation; lack of advantage or disadvantage.

ZE: 澤 *marsh, swamp*: one of the four types of land; analogy for uncertain situations.

ZHAN: 戰 *battle*: meeting an opponent or challenge; literally "big weapon;" not necessarily fighting, as in the idea of conflict, ZHENG.

ZHENG: 爭 *conflict, contentious, disputed*: direct confrontation of arms; the nature of highly desirable ground; one of nine types of DI, terrain or situations.

ZHI: 知 *know, knowledge*: to understand or comprehend; the basis of all other skills; the foundation of success.

ZHII: 支 *support, supporting*: to prop up; to enhance; one of six field positions; the opposite extreme of GUA, entangling.

ZHUAN: 專 *concentrate, focus*: the process of bringing resources together for a single purpose; the opposite of FEN, divide.

ZI: 輜 *supply wagons*: the transportation of supplies; one of the five targets of fire attacks.

ZONG: 眾 *crowd*: large group of people; a strong concentration of forces at a certain position; the opposite of SHOA, few.

Index of Topics in *The Art of War*

This index identifies significant topics, keyed to the chapters, block numbers (big numbers in text), and line numbers (tiny numbers). The format is chapter:block.lines.

An Invitation to Martial Arts Trainers

If you currently teach the martial arts, we would like to invite you to join the Science of Strategy Institute as a trainer teaching your students the lost secrets of the *Bing-fa*. This training in martial arts strategy is the perfect intellectual complement to the physical training you already provide. The principles of strategy will prepare your students to utilize the lessons of the martial arts in their everyday lives. Join our worldwide network of licensed trainers, and we will provide you with all the training materials that you need.

The Institute's programs will help your students reach their true potential. Without this training, people respond to life's challenges instinctively, either running away from them or getting into unnecessary battles. Once your students master these lessons, they will respond to challenges by looking for strategic opportunities. Solidly grounded in the original philosophy of the martial arts, our books and training materials are designed to be practical, entertaining, and enlightening.

You can also use our training material to promote your martial arts training business in your community. The martial arts are unique in that they are based on a sophisticated competitive philosophy that is interesting to broad segments of the community. We can show you, as one of our trainers, how to leverage that interest and create thousands of dollars of free publicity for your business.

The Science of Strategy Institute is an international organization dedicated teaching the principles of strategy. We have licensed trainers all over the world. Our guiding principle is to popularize the knowledge of classical strategy that came down to us from the *Sunzi Bing-fa*, also known as Sun Tzu's *The Art of War*.

FOR A SPECIAL OFFER AVAILABLE ONLY TO OWNERS OF THIS BOOK, GO TO

www.scienceofstrategy.com/martial-arts-training.htm

Science of Strategy Institute
PO Box 19542
Seattle, WA 98133

JOIN THE SCIENCE OF STRATEGY INSTITUTE
WWW.SCIENCEOFSTRATEGY.COM

BECOME THE COMPLETE STRATEGIST!

BOOK PROGRAMS
Library Memberships
Book Club Memberships
Books and Audios

ON-LINE TRAINING PROGRAMS
The Warrior Class
The Strategy School

ACADEMY OF STRATEGY
On-line Training
The Academy Library
Personalized Advice on Strategy

INSTITUTE SEMINARS AND TRAINING
A Worldwide Network of Trainers
Internal Corporate Licensing

About the Author

Gary Gagliardi, the founder of the Science of Strategy Institute, is the award-winning author of over a dozen books on strategy and Chinese culture, who has trained the world's largest organizations. Visit **www.scienceofstrategy.com** to learn more about his books and seminar programs.